C000153466

Microsoft Office 2000
explained

Books Available

By both authors:

BP327 DOS one step at a time
BP337 A Concise User's Guide to Lotus 1-2-3 for Windows
BP341 MS-DOS explained
BP346 Programming in Visual Basic for Windows
BP352 Excel 5 explained
BP362 Access one step at a time
BP387 Windows one step at a time
BP388 Why not personalise your PC
BP400 Windows 95 explained
BP406 MS Word 95 explained
BP407 Excel 95 explained
BP408 Access 95 one step at a time
BP409 MS Office 95 one step at a time
BP415 Using Netscape on the Internet*
BP420 E-mail on the Internet*
BP426 MS-Office 97 explained
BP428 MS-Word 97 explained
BP429 MS-Excel 97 explained
BP430 MS-Access 97 one step at a time
BP433 Your own Web site on the Internet
BP448 Lotus SmartSuite 97 explained
BP456 Windows 98 explained*
BP460 Using Microsoft Explorer 4 on the Internet*
BP464 E-mail and news with Outlook Express*
BP465 Lotus SmartSuite Millennium explained
BP471 Microsoft Office 2000 explained
BP472 Microsoft Word 2000 explained
BP473 Microsoft Excel 2000 explained
BP474 Microsoft Access 2000 explained
BP478 Microsoft Works 2000 explained

By Noel Kantaris:

BP258 Learning to Program in C
BP259 A Concise Introduction to UNIX*
BP284 Programming in QuickBASIC
BP325 A Concise User's Guide to Windows 3.1

Microsoft Office 2000 explained

by

N. Kantaris
and
P.R.M. Oliver

Bernard Babani (publishing) Ltd
The Grampians
Shepherds Bush Road
London W6 7NF
England

Please Note

Although every care has been taken with the production of this book to ensure that any projects, designs, modifications and/or programs, etc., contained herewith, operate in a correct and safe manner and also that any components specified are normally available in Great Britain, the Publishers and Author(s) do not accept responsibility in any way for the failure (including fault in design) of any project, design, modification or program to work correctly or to cause damage to any equipment that it may be connected to or used in conjunction with, or in respect of any other damage or injury that may be so caused, nor do the Publishers accept responsibility in any way for the failure to obtain specified components.

Notice is also given that if equipment that is still under warranty is modified in any way or used or connected with home-built equipment then that warranty may be void.

First Published - September 1999

British Library Cataloguing in Publication Data:

A catalogue record for this book is available from the British Library

ISBN 0 85934 471 1

Cover Design by Gregor Arthur
Cover illustration by Adam Willis
Printed and Bound in Great Britain by Bath Press, Bath

About this Book

Microsoft Office 2000 explained has been written to help users to get to grips with the integrated components of this package, namely, the e-mail and desktop manager *Outlook*, the word processor *Word*, the spreadsheet *Excel*, the presentation graphics *PowerPoint*, the database *Access*, and the *Microsoft Publisher*. The latter is bundled with three of the four *Microsoft Office 2000* sets, but excluded from the *Standard* edition. All these components were specifically designed for the *Windows 95/98, 2000*, and *NT* environments.

The book does not describe how to install and use Microsoft Windows. If you need to know more about Windows, then may we suggest you select an appropriate level book for your needs from the 'Books Available' list - the books are loosely graduated in complexity with the less demanding *One step at a time* series, to the more detailed *Explained* series. They are all published by BERNARD BABANI (publishing) Ltd.

The individual applications which make up *Microsoft Office 2000* are designed to work together and have the same look and feel, which makes it easy to learn. For example, the majority of menus, toolbar buttons, and dialogue boxes are the same in each application, which gives them a consistent user interface.

The package improves on previous Office capabilities with the improved use of the

- Office Assistant - the online, natural language interface which assist you with the tasks in hand.

- Command Bars - the enhanced user interface which provides a unified system of toolbars and menus across all applications of Office 2000.

- Multilingual Features - Office 2000 programs support editing and viewing of documents in more than 80 languages.

- Automatic Language Detection - the English (U.S.) version of Office 2000 comes with proofing tools for English, Spanish, and French.

- Office Tools - the consistent interface to a number of graphics and drawing facilities across Word, Excel, and PowerPoint.

- Outlook 2000 - the application that helps users to manage e-mail, contact lists, calendars, to do lists, and documents.

- IntelliSense - the features which help you with your work, no matter which application you are using.

Microsoft Office 2000 is an exciting new Office suite that will help you with the new millennium challenges and opportunities to business. It offers new tools that use Web technology to provide enhanced workgroup productivity and the ability to access and analyse important business data more efficiently. *Microsoft Office 2000* also provides new levels of intelligence and integration, making it much easier to use than before.

The various applications within *Microsoft Office 2000* can either be used by themselves or made to share information. This book introduces each application by itself, with sufficient detail to get you working, then discusses how to share information between them. No prior knowledge of this package's applications is assumed.

The book was written with the busy person in mind. It is not necessary to learn all there is to know about a subject, when reading a few selected pages can usually do the same thing quite adequately. With the help of this book, it is hoped that you will be able to come to terms with Microsoft Office and get the most out of your computer in terms of efficiency, productivity and enjoyment, and that you will be able to do it in the shortest, most effective and informative way.

If you would like to purchase a Companion Disc for any of the listed books by the same author(s), apart from the ones marked with an asterisk, containing the file/program listings which appear in them, then fill in the form at the back of the book and send it to Phil Oliver at the stipulated address.

About the Authors

Noel Kantaris graduated in Electrical Engineering at Bristol University and after spending three years in the Electronics Industry in London, took up a Tutorship in Physics at the University of Queensland. Research interests in Ionospheric Physics, led to the degrees of M.E. in Electronics and Ph.D. in Physics. On return to the UK, he took up a Post-Doctoral Research Fellowship in Radio Physics at the University of Leicester, and then in 1973 a lecturing position in Engineering at the Camborne School of Mines, Cornwall, (part of Exeter University), where between 1978 and 1997 he was also the CSM Computing Manager. At present he is IT Director of FFC Ltd.

Phil Oliver graduated in Mining Engineering at Camborne School of Mines in 1967 and since then has specialised in most aspects of surface mining technology, with a particular emphasis on computer related techniques. He has worked in Guyana, Canada, several Middle Eastern countries, South Africa and the United Kingdom, on such diverse projects as: the planning and management of bauxite, iron, gold and coal mines; rock excavation contracting in the UK; international mining equipment sales and international mine consulting for a major mining house in South Africa. In 1988 he took up a lecturing position at Camborne School of Mines (part of Exeter University) in Surface Mining and Management. He retired from full-time lecturing in 1998, to spend more time writing, consulting and developing Web sites for clients.

Acknowledgements

We would like to thank the staff of Text 100 Limited for providing the software programs on which this work was based. We would also like to thank colleagues at the Camborne School of Mines for the helpful tips and suggestions which assisted us in the writing of this book.

Trademarks

Arial and **Times New Roman** are registered trademarks of The Monotype Corporation plc.

HP and LaserJet are registered trademarks of Hewlett Packard Corporation.

IBM is a registered trademark of International Business Machines, Inc.

Intel is a registered trademark of Intel Corporation.

Microsoft, **MS-DOS**, **Windows**, **Windows NT**, and **Visual Basic**, are either registered trademarks or trademarks of Microsoft Corporation.

PostScript is a registered trademark of Adobe Systems Incorporated.

TrueType is a registered trademark of Apple Corporation.

All other brand and product names used in the book are recognised as trademarks, or registered trademarks, of their respective companies.

Contents

1

Package Overview

Microsoft Office 2000 is a collection of powerful, full-featured, programs with the same look and feel that work together as if they were a single program. Office 2000 was specifically designed to allow you to work with your information data, either by yourself or to share such data with others, if you so wish, quickly and efficiently.

Microsoft Office 2000 comes in four flavours, each one of which contains a different mixture of applications (for an explanation on what these applications can do, see overleaf). The four sets are: Premium with 9 applications, Professional with 7 applications, Small Business with 5 applications, and Standard with 4 applications. The various mixtures of applications for these four packages are as follows:

Office 2000 Unique Sets	Office 2000 Applications								
	Outlook	Word	Excel	PowerPoint	Access	Publisher	Small Bus. Tools	FrontPage	PhotoDraw
Premium	☺	☺	☺	☺	☺	☺	☺	☺	☺
Professional	☺	☺	☺	☺	☺	☺	☺		
Small Business	☺	☺	☺			☺	☺		
Standard	☺	☺	☺	☺					

The various Office 2000 applications have the following main functions:

Outlook   E-mail and Personal Information Manager (PIM) - provides a full set of multi-user, group-scheduling PIM functions, including a multi-account e-mail client.

Word   Word processor - offers almost every imaginable feature, including background spell and grammar checking, integrated drawing tools, four WYSIWYG editing views, and Web site creation.

Excel   Electronic spreadsheet - allows the creation of a 3D super-spreadsheet by using multi-page workbooks which support 3D *drill-through* formulae, and includes a long list of 'goal-seeking', 'what-if?' analysis tools and an excellent set of database capabilities.

PowerPoint   Presentation graphics - allows creation of slide shows for training, sales and other presentations, and includes, amongst other capabilities, object animation, speaker notes, and recorded voice-overs.

Access   Database management - includes a full set of WYSIWYG design tools for database, forms, queries and reports, plus a full Visual Basic derived programming language for developing specific applications.

Publisher   Desktop publishing - allows the design and creation of printed documents with the help of 2,000 publication templates. It allows you to auto-fit text to frame sizes, provides inter-frame text flow options, and auto-wraps text around irregular images.

S B Tools   Small Business Tools and customer management - allows users to understand their customer base better by providing account tracking and analysis tools.

FrontPage   Web site publishing - gives users tools to create and manage Web sites, whether personal or corporate Web pages on intranet or Internet sites.

PhotoDraw Business graphics - combines powerful photo-editing and drawing in one easy to use application to enable business users to create professional looking graphics for printed material and Web pages.

All Office 2000 applications have a built-in consistency which makes them easier to use. For example, they all have standardised toolbars and consistent menus, commands, and dialogue boxes. Once you become familiar with one application, it is far easier to learn and use the others.

Microsoft Office 2000 applications are the most integrated to date. Just like its predecessor, Office 2000 applications make use of what is known as IntelliSense, which anticipates what you want to do and produces the correct result. For example, AutoCorrect, AutoFormat, and AutoComplete in Word can, when activated, automatically correct common spelling mistakes, format an entire document, or complete the word you are typing.

Amongst other common code, first introduced in Office 95, then improved in Office 97, are the Wizards which can help you simplify everyday and/or complex tasks, and the support for the Microsoft Visual Basic for Applications, which gives you a powerful and flexible development platform with which to create custom solutions.

Office 2000 comes with several new cross-application themes which are implemented across most, but not all, the applications in the suite. These offer the following facilities:

- **Installation** - unlike previous versions of Office where components of applications could be added when required by running the Install program, Office 2000 provides two ways of installation per component: (i) run from the CD, or (ii) install on First Use (also known as install on Demand).

However, running an Office component from the CD is rather a slow process, but it does save on valuable space on your hard disc. The second option, install on First Use, might appear at first to be similar to that of previous versions of the suite, but for one difference; the omitted components still appear on the Office's menus. The first time you attempt to use such a menu option causes the Install program to interrupt your work and ask you for the CD in order to install the missing component. To avoid such interruptions, you could install all of the program's features at the beginning.

- **HTML file formats** - Office 2000 has elevated its previous version of the HTML file format to a 'companion' document format for Word, Excel, and PowerPoint. You can now have file open/save access direct to compatible Web servers, making a Web site design very easy indeed. Other users can see such Web pages even though they might not have these applications installed.

  Files created in a companion HTML format store the documents' application specific information in XML (Extended Markup Language). This allows the originator to open such files in their original application, edit them, and save them back onto their Web site. However, the source of such code cannot be edited manually, as even the simplest of documents contains endless lines of XML and style sheet code, making the actual content difficult to find.

- **Toolbar and menu behaviour** - the changes in this aspect of the suite-wide user interface has been improved. Pressing a toolbar button in any of the Office 2000 applications now opens a drop-down menu with only the most important options shown, but with the option to view the full menu. Furthermore, Office 2000 learns from your actions, automatically promoting the items you choose from menu extensions on to the shortened version of the menu. Although this moving around of menu options might cause confusion to the inexperienced user, it is nevertheless quite effective.

- **Switching between documents** - unlike previous versions of Office applications where switching between documents could only be achieved by using the **Window** command and selecting the appropriate document, Office 2000 introduces a hybrid system. You can still use the old method of selecting the required document, but now each document opened in an application, places a button on the Taskbar. Switching between multiple documents can now be done easily and quickly by left-clicking on the appropriate Taskbar button, provided you only have few documents to choose from. As the number of opened documents increases, the size of the buttons on the Taskbar shrink to accommodate them which makes it difficult to distinguish between them.

  However, different applications within Office 2000 behave differently when displaying multiple documents. For example, Word opens each document into its own application window, while Excel, PowerPoint, and Access open multiple documents within a single application window. All of the above mentioned applications place document buttons on the Taskbar, but Access places a button for each table, form, query, or table opened from a single database. Other applications, such as FrontPage and PhotoDraw, retain the old style single button multi-document interface.

- **Office Assistant** - The animated online natural language help first introduced in Office 97, now has the ability of jumping out of the way of your work. However, it manages to get in the way of the Office 2000 help screens (pressing **F1** does not activate the applications Help window if the Assistant is turned on). Luckily, you can turn the Assistant off by right-clicking on it, and selecting **Options** from the displayed quick menu which opens the Office Assistant dialogue box, then unchecking the **Use the Office Assistant** option. To reactivate the Office Assistant, use the **Help**, **Show the Office Assistant** command. More about this later.

Hardware and Software Requirements

If Microsoft Office is already installed on your computer, you can safely skip this and the next section of this chapter.

To install and use Microsoft Office 2000, you need an IBM-compatible PC equipped with Intel's Pentium processor. Microsoft suggests a 166 MHz processor if you intend to use PhotoDraw, otherwise a 75 MHz processor is quite adequate. In addition, you need the following:

* Windows 95/98 (or higher), or Windows NT as the operating system.

* Random access memory (RAM) required is:

  For Windows 9x or higher, 16 MB plus 4 MB for each running application (8 MB for Outlook, Access or FrontPage).

  For Windows NT, 32 MB plus what is needed to run the applications as specified above.

* Hard disc space required for Microsoft Office 2000 is:

  Standard edition; 189 MB.

  Small Business edition; 178 MB (for Outlook, Word, and Excel), plus an additional 182 MB (for Publisher and Small Business Tools).

  Professional edition: 217 MB (for Outlook, Word, Excel, PowerPoint, and Access), plus an additional 174 MB (for Publisher and Small Business Tools).

  Premium edition: 252 MB (for Outlook, Word, Excel, PowerPoint, Access, and FrontPage), plus 174 MB (for Publisher and Small Business Tools), plus 100 MB (for PhotoDraw).

* CD-ROM drive.

* Video adapter: VGA or higher resolution. If you are using PowerPoint or PhotoDraw, you will need a 256-colour video adapter or higher.

* Pointing device: Microsoft Mouse or compatible.

Realistically, to run Office 2000 Pro with reasonable sized applications, you will need a 100 MHz Pentium PC with at least 32 MB of RAM. To run Microsoft Office 2000 from a network, you must also have a network compatible with your Windows operating environment, such as Microsoft's Windows 95/98 or higher, Windows NT, LAN Manager, etc.

Finally, if you are connected to the Internet, you can take advantage of Word's advanced editing and formatting features when working with e-mail messages. Word can be used as an alternate e-mail editor for Outlook and Outlook Express, and now takes advantage of custom backgrounds and themes, as well as supporting auto signatures. However, before you can do so, you must have Outlook or Outlook Express installed on your computer and in that program have Word 2000 selected as your e-mail editor.

Installing Microsoft Office 2000

Installing Office on your computer's hard disc is made very easy using the SETUP program, which even configures Office automatically to take advantage of the computer's hardware. One of SETUP's functions is to convert compressed Office files from the CD-ROM, prior to copying them onto your hard disc.

Note: If you are using a virus detection utility, disable it before running SETUP, as it might conflict with it.

To install Microsoft Office, place the distribution CD in your CD drive and close it. The auto-start program on the CD will start the SETUP program automatically. If that does not work, click the **Start** button, and select the **Run** command which opens the Run dialogue box, as shown below.

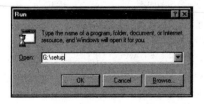

Next, type in the **Command Line** box:

    g:\setup

In our case we used the CD-ROM in the G: drive; yours could be different.

Clicking the **OK** button, starts the installation of Microsoft Office 2000. SETUP displays the following screen:

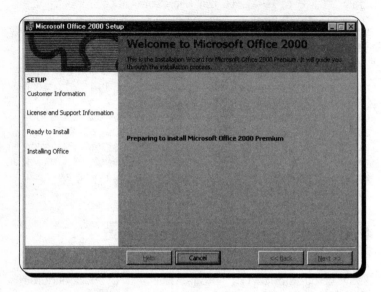

We suggest that you follow the instructions displayed on the screen. Clicking the **Next** button, causes SETUP to go through the following procedure:

- Prompts you to type your name and the name of your organisation (optional).

- Prompts you to type in the Product Key.

- Asks you to accept the licence agreement.

- Prompts you to supply the path to the directory where you want to install Office, and then checks your system and the available hard disc space.

- Searches your system's discs for installed Office components and asks you whether older versions of Office applications should be removed or not.

- Asks you to specify which Office features you require by displaying the following screen.

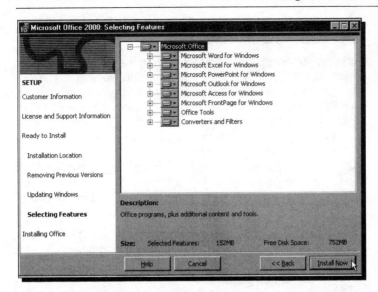

The symbol next to the feature indicates how the feature is installed by default. The symbols and their meanings are as shown below.

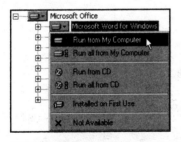

You can change how the feature is installed by clicking its symbol and then selecting another symbol from the list that appears. If a feature has sub-features, a symbol with a white background indicates that the feature and all of its sub-features have the same installation method. A symbol with a grey background indicates that the feature and its sub-features have mixed installation methods.

When you have made all of your installation choices, click **Install Now** to begin the installation.

The Office Shortcut Bar

During installation, the Office Shortcut Bar is collated and added to the Windows Start Up program so that it will be displayed automatically on your screen whenever you start your PC. The contents of a Microsoft Shortcut Bar which you might have assembled will be preserved. The Shortcut Bar will be displayed when you restart your computer.

The Microsoft Office Shortcut Bar, provides a convenient way to work with your documents and the Office applications by complementing the Windows **Start** menu.

The buttons on the Shortcut Bar of Office 2000 Professional edition, have the following labels:

New Office Document

Open Office Document

Microsoft Word

Microsoft Excel

Microsoft PowerPoint

Microsoft Outlook

Microsoft Access

Screen Saver

Microsoft Publisher

New Appointment

New Contact

New Journal Entry

New Message

New Note

New Task

Apart from the buttons which launch the four main applications in Office 2000 (Word, Excel, PowerPoint, and Access), the function of the other buttons is as follows:

New Office Document: Allows you to select in the displayed dialogue box the tab containing the type of document you want to work with. Double-clicking the type of document or template you want, automatically loads the appropriate application.

Open Office Document: Allows you to work with an existing document. Opening a document, first starts the application originally used to create it.

Microsoft Outlook: Launches the desktop manager used to manage your e-mail, contact lists, tasks and documents.

Screen Saver: Activates instantly your screen saver.

Microsoft FrontPage: Launches the Web design program.

New Appointment: Allows you to add a new appointment in your management system. This caters for all-day or multiple-day events and a meeting planner, including meeting request processing and attendance lists.

New Contact: Allows you to enter a new contact in Outlook's database, or to send an e-mail message direct from the contact manager and use hyper-links for direct access to a contact's home page on the Internet.

New Journal Entry: Allows you to make a New Journal.

New Message: Allows you to type a New Message.

New Note: Allows you to type a new Note.

New Task: Allows you to add a new task in your management system, including automatic composition of an e-mail message summarising a task and automatic tracking of tasks sent to other users.

During installation, Office 2000 adds Outlook Express 5 button on the 'Quick Start' area of the Windows Task bar (next to the **Start** button). A single click of the left mouse button launches this application.

Adding or Removing Office Applications

To add or remove an Office application, left-click the **Start** button at the bottom left corner of the screen, point to **Settings**, then click the **Control Panel** option on the Windows pop-up menu, as shown below.

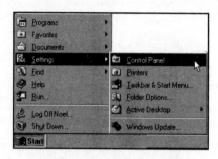

This opens the Control Panel dialogue box. Next, double-click the Add/Remove Programs icon, 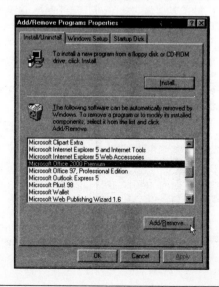 shown here to the left, to open the dialogue box below. Click the Install/Uninstall tab and select the Microsoft Office 2000 program, and then click the **Add/Remove** button.

This requires you insert the Office 2000 CD into your CD drive, which causes SETUP to display the following Maintenance Mode dialogue box:

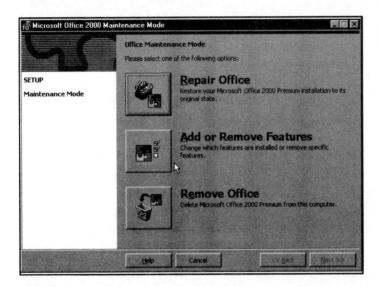

Selecting the **A̱dd or Remove Features** opens up the

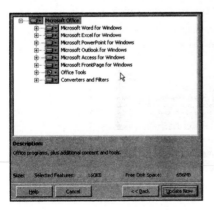

dialogue box to the left which is identical to that shown on page 9 where we discussed how you can add or remove Office features.

Note the additional buttons on the above screen. Use the **Repair Office** button to reinstall the whole of Office 2000, or to find and fix any errors in your original installation. Finally, you can use the **Re̱move Office** button to uninstall all of the Office 2000 applications.

Changing the Office Shortcut Bar

You have the option of changing the buttons on the Office Shortcut Bar. To do so, left-click on an empty part of the Shortcut bar to display the available options, as shown here to the left.

Here, we show the 'Programs' option ticked, which we find most useful for quickly launching a selection of programs. Clicking this option, replaces the original Office Shortcut Bar with the one shown here to the right. However, clicking the Office icon (top left), changes the Shortcut Bar back to the original Office Shortcut Bar. In this way, you can flick between selected Shortcut Bars.

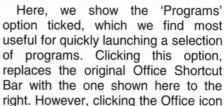

Adding/Deleting Buttons

You can add buttons to the Shortcut Bar by dragging them there. To find the application you want to add to this bar, use the Windows **Start**, **Find** command.

To delete a button, right-click on an empty part of the Shortcut Bar, select **Customize** from the displayed menu, then click the Buttons tab, select the unwanted button and click **Delete**. But beware, this also deletes the folder that holds the application! It may be better to hide it.

Hiding/Displaying Buttons

To hide a button from the Shortcut Bar (without deleting it), right-click on the button and select the **Hide Button** option on the displayed menu, shown here to the left. To display previously hidden buttons, right-click the Shortcut Bar, use the **Customize** option on the displayed menu and click the Button tab. Clicking on the check box of the required button makes it visible on the Shortcut Bar. Clicking again, clears its check mark and hides it.

The Mouse Pointers

In Office 2000 applications, as with all other graphical based programs, the use of a mouse makes many operations both easier and more fun to carry out.

Office 2000 makes use of the mouse pointers available in Windows, some of the most common of which are illustrated below. When an Office application is initially started up the first you will see is the hourglass, which turns into an upward pointing hollow arrow once the individual application screen appears on your display. Other shapes depend on the type of work you are doing at the time.

 The hourglass which displays when you are waiting while performing a function.

 The arrow which appears when the pointer is placed over menus, scrolling bars, and buttons.

I The I-beam which appears in normal text areas of the screen. For additional 'Click and Type' pointer shapes, specific to Office 2000 applications, see the table overleaf.

 The 4-headed arrow which appears when you choose to move a table, a chart area, or a frame.

 The double arrows which appear when over the border of a window, used to drag the side and alter the size of the window.

 The Help hand which appears in the Help windows, and is used to access 'hypertext' type links.

Office 2000 applications, like other Windows packages, have additional mouse pointers which facilitate the execution of selected commands. Some of these are:

↓   The vertical pointer which appears when pointing over a column in a table or worksheet and used to select the column.

➡   The horizontal pointer which appears when pointing at a row in a table or worksheet and used to select the row.

↗   The slanted arrow which appears when the pointer is placed in the selection bar area of text or a table.

↔   The vertical split arrow which appears when pointing over the area separating two columns and used to size a column.

↕   The horizontal split arrow which appears when pointing over the area separating two rows and used to size a row.

+   The cross which you drag to extend or fill a series.

✎   The draw pointer which appears when you are drawing freehand.

Word 2000 introduces the following Click and Type pointer shapes which appear as you move the I-beam pointer into a specific formatting zone; their shape indicating which formatting will apply when you double-click.

I≡	Align left	≡I	Align right
I≣	Centre	I≣	Left indent
I≣	Left text wrap	≣I	Right text wrap

If you don't see the Click and Type pointer shape, check that the facility is turned on. You can do this by using the **Tools**, **Options** command, then click the Edit tab and select the **Enable click and type** check box, and press **OK**.

Using the Office Assistant

The Office Assistant is a central source of application information. No matter which Office 2000 application you are using, the Assistant is there to help you.

To find out how it works, start one of the Office applications (we have used Word), then click the relevant Office Assistant button, shown here, with

the left mouse button, type the word *help* in the displayed 'What would you like to do?' box, shown to the left, and left-click the **Search** button.

A list of help topics is then displayed, as shown to the right. To see more topics, left-click the small triangle at the bottom of the list with the caption 'See more', to display additional topics, as shown below.

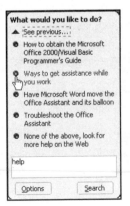

To find out how you can use the Office Assistant, click the 'Ways to get assistance while you work' option which causes the display of the screen shown on the next page. From this latter screen you can find out all there is to know about the Office Assistant.

The very same screen can be displayed from all Office applications, with only the title of the window and the 'Finding out what's new in ...' hypertext link, changing to reflect the application in use.

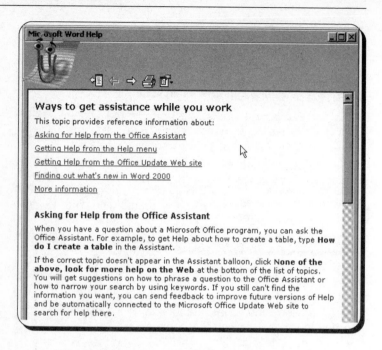

Note the Web browser type buttons at the top of the screen. These allow you to carry out the following functions:

<img>	**Show** - click this button to display the help screen tabs which allow you to access Help's Contents, Answer Wizard, and Index.
<img>	**Back** - if more than one help screen has been opened, click this button to go back to the previously opened help screen.
<img>	**Forward** - if you have moved back to a previous help screen, click this button to move forward through opened help screens.
<img>	**Print** - click this button to print the contents of the current help screen.
<img>	**Options** - click this button to open up a menu of options which control all of the above facilities plus the ability to select the Internet Options dialogue box.

Customising the Office Assistant

You can customise the Office Assistant to a great degree. Not only can you change the way it responds to your enquiries, but you can even switch it off once you have mastered a particular Office application.

To see the default options settings of the Office Assistant, activate it, left-click on it, and left-click the **Options** button on the displayed box, shown here.

Doing this, causes the following dialogue box to be displayed on your screen:

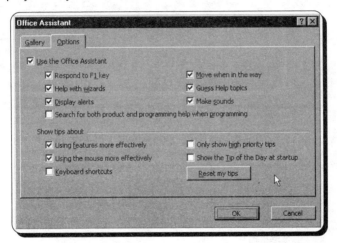

As you can see, it is possible to choose from several options. Should you like to change the shape of your Office Assistant (there are eight shapes to choose from - see next page), either left-click the Gallery tab of the above dialogue box, or right-click the Office Assistant and select the **Choose Assistant** option from the displayed menu, as shown here.

Either action displays the following dialogue box in which you can select your preferred Assistant shape by left-clicking the **<u>N</u>ext** button.

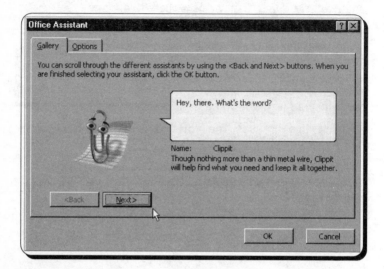

The shapes of the available Assistants are as follows:

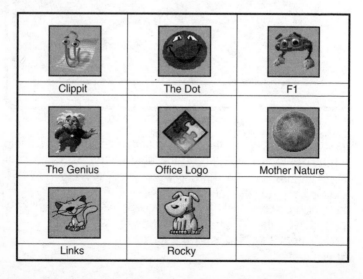

Clippit	The Dot	F1
The Genius	Office Logo	Mother Nature
Links	Rocky	

Using the Help Menu

Another way of getting help in an
Office application is to use the **F1**
function key to get directly to the
Context and Index help screens.
To do so, however, you will have
to switch off the Office Assistant
first by right-clicking it and
selecting **Options** from the
drop-down menu. This opens the
following dialogue box, in which you must clear the box
against <u>U</u>se the Office Assistant, as shown below.

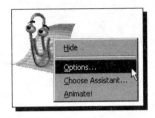

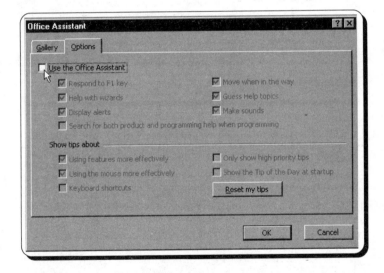

Next time you press the **F1** function key, the Office Help
screen appears as shown on the next page. You can either
view information on the screen or print it on paper.
Left-clicking the Index tab, displays a dialogue box with three
areas for typing, selecting and displaying information, as
shown.

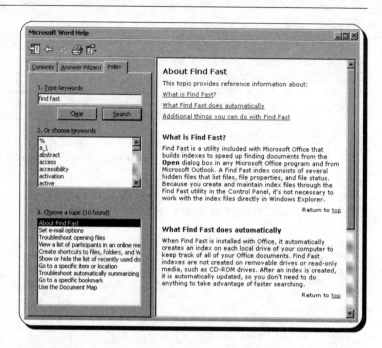

Typing, for example, the words ***find fast*** in the first 'Type keywords' box, causes a list of related topics to appear automatically in the second 'Or choose key words' box. Selection of one or more matching words from the displayed list narrows down the selection of topics appearing in the third 'Choose a topic' box. Finally, selecting a topic from the third display box by left-clicking it, displays information on your selection.

If the keyword you want to choose is not visible within the display area of the second box, use the scroll bar to get to it.

As an exercise, click the Answer Wizard tab of the Help dialogue box and type the words 'backward compatibility' in the 'What would you like to do' box and click the **Search** button. Immediately the topic 'Results of saving Word 2000 documents in other formats' appears highlighted at the top of the list in the second text box, as shown on the next page. As each topic in this list is selected, information about it is automatically displayed in the adjacent text box.

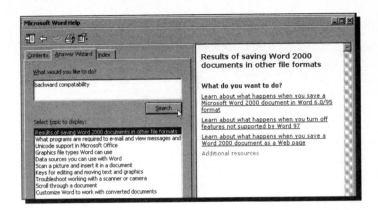

Next, left-click the first item to display all you need to know, in this instance, about the Word 2000, 95, and 6.0 file formats. Similar searches carried out from other Office 2000 applications will reveal what you should do if you require backward compatibility.

It is worth while exploring the different ways in which you can get help with or without the Office Assistant. For

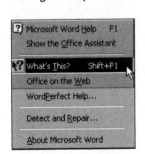

example, another way of getting context sensitive help is to select the '**What's This**' option from the extended **Help** sub-menu, then move the modified mouse pointer to an area of the document, or onto a particular Toolbar button, and press the left mouse button.

Finally, click the Contents tab of the Help screen to open up an impressive list of topics relating to the particular Office application you are using. Left-clicking a selected book, displays the topics and other books it might contain. As each topic is selected, information about that topic appears on the adjacent screen, as shown overleaf.

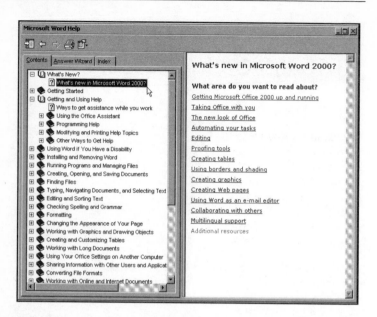

Note the small '+' signs to the left of each book. Left-clicking this sign, opens up the relevant book, indicated by a '-' sign. Do spend some time here to learn, particularly what is new in an application. Other topics can always be explored later.

2

Microsoft Outlook 2000

Microsoft's Outlook 2000 is a powerful personal information manager (PIM) that supports a full set of multi-user, group scheduling PIM functions. Outlook 2000 can be made the centre of activity for all the other Office 2000 applications; it can be used *online* or *off-line*. Outlook now includes a multiple-account e-mail client, compatible with Microsoft's Exchange messaging server as well as Internet-based POP3 and IMAG mail systems.

To work online, your computer must be connected to a shared network resource, which is imperative if you are planning to use Outlook's group-scheduling features. In that case, your computer must have a connection to a *post office* which is a list of Mail users on the system. Outlook 2000 can do the following:

- Manage information such as your appointments, contacts, tasks, and files, and if your computer is connected to a network, manage your e-mail, use group scheduling, and public folders.

- Browse and find Office files from within Outlook.

- Share information across the World Wide Web, provided you are connected to the Internet and have a browser, such as Microsoft's Explorer or Netscape.

A major example of integration of Outlook 2000 with the rest of the Office suite is the Journal, which automatically tracks use of the other Office applications. It can be customised to monitor as many or as few entries of activity as required, for example, to record an entry every time you open, save or print a document from any of Office 2000's applications. The result can be a time map of the user's day's or week's activity.

Starting Microsoft Outlook 2000

Outlook 2000 is started in Windows either by clicking on the 'Microsoft Outlook' icon on the Office Shortcut Bar, or by

clicking any of the six icons 'New Appointment' 'New Contact', 'New Journal Entry', 'New Message', 'New Note', or 'NewTask', also to be found on the Office Shortcut Bar. Once you have created an Outlook file, you can also start the program by clicking the 'Open Office Document' icon on the Office Shortcut Bar and double-clicking the relevant Outlook file.

If you are not using the Office Shortcut Bar, then you can start Outlook 2000 by clicking the Windows **Start** button, selecting **Programs** and then clicking on the 'Microsoft Outlook 2000' icon on the cascade menu.

When you start Outlook 2000 the program momentarily displays its opening screen, shown below, and then displays the Personal Folders screen shown on the next page.

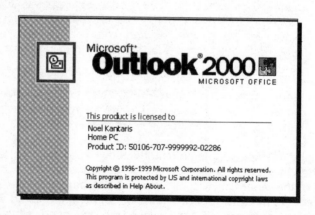

If the Office Assistant is activated, search for 'help', in which case it will open the Help list shown on the same screen dump at the top of the next page.

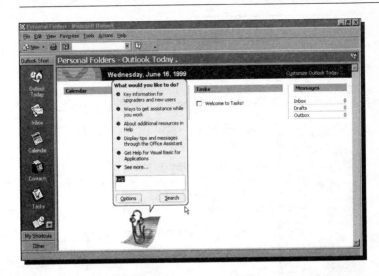

We suggest that you spend some time looking at all the items on the Help List, starting with the 'Key information for upgraders and new users', which will display additional topics on the screen as follows:

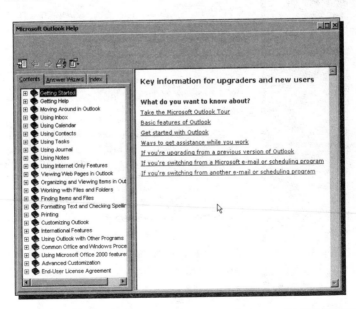

Managing Information

You can use Outlook to effectively manage information whether it is personal or business. The Outlook screen provides you with the means to manage information on three general topics: Outlook Shortcuts, My Shortcuts, and Other.

Outlook Shortcuts provides the following tools:

Outlook Today - gives you a snapshot of your day. It lists your appointments for the week, your tasks, and how many new e-mail messages you have.

Inbox - used to send and receive messages, preview messages before you open them, and manage your e-mail folders (see next chapter).

Calendar - used to keep track of your schedule and plan meetings with others. Use the TaskPad to see the day's tasks.

Contacts - used to keep your personal and business contact information up-to-date. Sort and file contacts any way you want, and go directly to their Web page.

Tasks - used to organise your personal and business to-do list in one easy-to-manage place.

Journal - used to record Outlook items, such as e-mail messages and files that are important, and to record and track activities of all types.

Notes - used to write down notes on anything you like, or drop text in notes that you want to reuse in other places.

Recycle bin - used to find deleted items and reinstate them.

My Shortcuts provides the following options:

Drafts - used to locate the folder in which unfinished messages have been saved.

Inbox - used to send and receive messages, preview messages before you open them, etc.

Sent Items - used to manage mail you have sent to others, a copy of which is saved in the sent items folder. Items can be sorted in any way you like.

Outbox - used to configure the way you send messages by delaying their delivery, or make them unavailable after a specified date.

Recycle bin - used to find deleted items and reinstate them.

Other provides the following tools:

My Computer - used to search drives and folders for a file you want to view, use, or perform housekeeping operations on, such as delete it or rename it.

My Documents - used to store Office documents, worksheets, databases, and presentations that you are working on inside the same folder.

Favorites - used to insert shortcuts to frequently used folders.

In general, you can use Outlook to open, view, and share other Office program files and use its various tools to help you work more efficiently.

Parts of the Outlook Screen

Before we go any further, take a look at the Outlook opening screen shown on page 27. The screen shows three distinct areas, **Calendar**, **Tasks** and **Messages**. Left-clicking any one of these, takes you to the appropriate option which can also be reached from the Outlook Option Bar (see below). Click the **Messages** option or the Inbox icon on the Outlook Option Bar, to display the following screen.

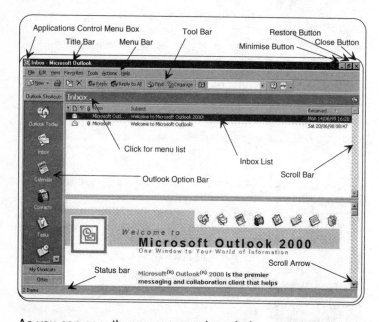

As you can see, there are several symbols which display on the Outlook screen. To find out what they are (they are too numerous to list here), highlight an item on the Inbox list and left-click the Assistant icon shown to the left, to display the help screen shown to the right. To see the list of symbols, left-click the first item on the Assistant's list. Try it, you need to know what they are.

Importing Information

If you already hold personal or business information, such as contacts or tasks to perform, on another program, now is the time to import these into Outlook.

To start the process, invoke the Assistant's help by typing 'Import data' in the **What would you like to do** text box. The screen to the right is then opened. To convert information, simply click the 'Import Information' button and follow the Wizard's instructions on the screen.

Below, we will attempt to import information from Schedule+ 7.0, our previously used scheduler. To do so, use the **File, Import and Export** command which opens the dialogue box below.

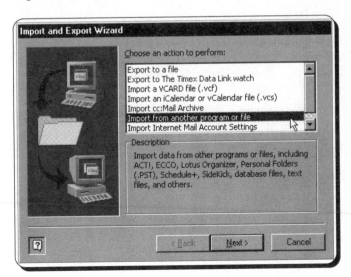

Clicking the **Next** button, causes the Wizard to display a list of possible organiser-type formats that it can handle by displaying the following screen.

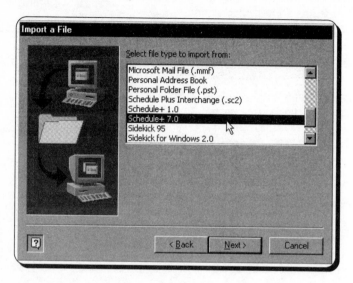

Selecting the type of file you want to convert and pressing the **Next** button starts the process. However, as the particular feature in Outlook 2000 was not originally installed on our computer, the following message was displayed:

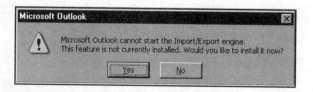

Pressing the **Yes** button causes the program to ask you to insert the Office 2000 CD in the CD-ROM drive, in order to install the missing feature.

After this is done, and after a short period the Import Wizard locates the old Schedule+ 7.0 files, as shown on the next page.

In our case the Wizard found the required file and proposes to carry out three actions, as detailed below. In your case these will most certainly be different.

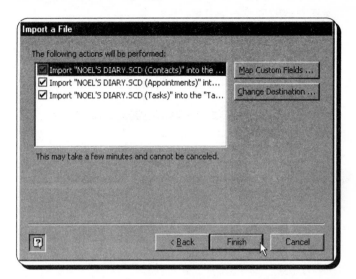

To find out what we have converted, click the Calendar, Contacts, and Tasks icon on Outlook Option Bar to display appropriate entries, provided they existed in your previous Scheduler. Below, we show our converted tasks.

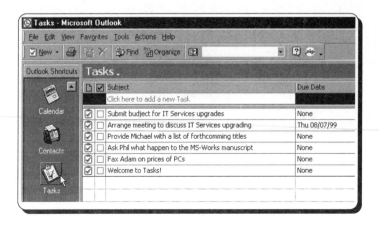

Using the Calendar

Before we start entering information in our Calendar, let us take a look at its opening screen.

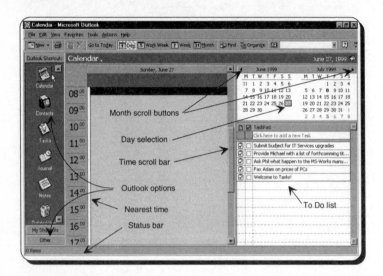

Viewing Appointments

When in Daily view, to look at another day, left-click on the day you want to look at on the monthly calendar at the top right of the screen.

To view a work week or a month at once, use the **View** command, then select **Work Week**, **Week** or **Month**, as shown to the left, or simply click the appropriate button on the Calendar Toolbar, shown below.

Whichever method you use the result is the same.

Clicking the monthly button, displays a typical, though almost empty, monthly diary, as shown below.

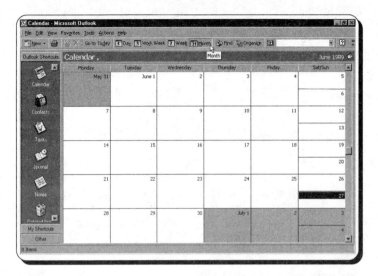

Changing the month you are viewing could not be simpler; just click the scroll buttons of the vertical scroll bar - clicking the upper scroll button displays earlier months, while clicking the lower scroll button displays later months.

All the details of appointments, events or meetings can be viewed in Outlook whether you are in the Daily, Weekly, or Monthly view; you can see the date, time, and the description. You also have the facility to use symbols to indicate whether the appointment is recurring, tentative, or private, and whether a reminder has been set, shown by a small bell, or other users have been invited (these will be discussed next).

Information relevant to an appointment or meeting is also displayed in the Appointment dialogue box (to see one, double-click on a day on the Calendar - again, this will be discussed next). To organise a meeting, however, you will need to click the Attendee Availability tab of the Appointment dialogue box.

Appointments, Meetings, and Events

Before you start scheduling an appointment, meeting or event, it is necessary to look at the following definitions:

- An appointment does not involve other colleagues or resources, and can be recurring, that is, it can be repeated on a regular basis.

- A meeting is an appointment that involves other people and possibly resources, and can also be recurring.

- An event is an activity that lasts one day, or more, such as attendance at an exhibition or conference. An annual event occurs yearly on a specific date. Events and annual events do not occupy blocks of time in your Calendar; instead, they appear as a banner below the current day heading.

Entering Appointments

To start with, let us type in a recurring appointment to, say, meet Section Managers, that takes place on Thursday every four weeks starting at 10:00 a.m. on 8 July and lasts for 2 hours. To do so, click on 8 July on the calendar to the right of the entry area, move the cursor to 10:00 a.m. and click the

Make a New Appointment icon, shown here. This opens the Appointment dialogue box displayed on the next page in which you can type 'Managers' meeting' in the **Subject** box, and 'My Office' in the **Location** box, set the **End time** to 12.00, click the **Reminder** box and select 15 minutes, and then press the **Recurrence** button on the Toolbar.

In the Appointment Recurrence dialogue box, click the **Weekly** radio button and in the **Recur every** box, pointed to by the mouse pointer on our screen dump, type '4', fill in the rest of the information as shown, and click **OK**. Finally, click the **Save and Close** button located at the top of the first dialogue box.

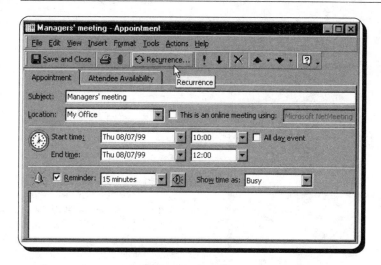

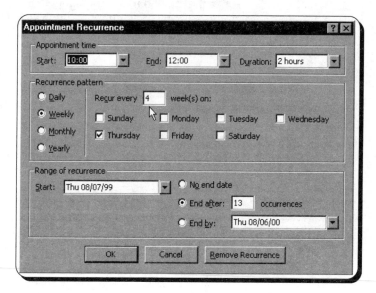

Your Calendar now shows the latest entry, including location

🔔 Managers' meeting (My Office)
↻

of meeting, together with the Reminder icon and the Recurring symbol.

If you want to make any changes to the newly created

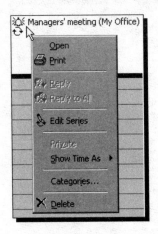

appointment, point to it and right-click it. You can use the options on this drop-down menu to print, edit, or delete the appointment. Choosing the **Edit Series** option, opens the Recurring Appointment dialogue box where you can make the required changes.

Next, let us now assume that you also have a special lunch appointment with your mother on the 5th of August each year, as it is her birthday. To enter this information click on 5 August on the calendar to the right of the Daily entry area, and create a yearly appointment 'Lunch with mother' for 1:00 p.m., for 1½ hours, as shown below. Add as a note the reminder 'Birthday lunch'.

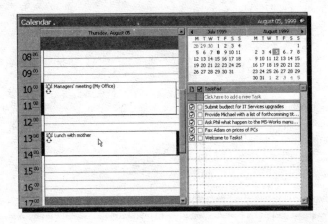

Note that the meeting with the Managers is also shown on the same day, as it is four weeks since the last meeting. This information also appears on the Weekly and the Monthly view. Try it!

Printing Information

Information held in a diary can be printed on paper. Simply use the **File, Print** command to open the dialogue box below.

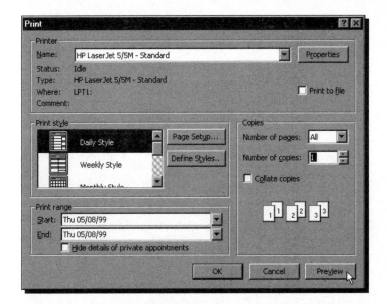

In the Printer **Name** box, at the top of the dialogue box, click the down arrow to select from one of the installed printers under Windows. Next, choose an appropriate item from the **Print Style** list and use the **Page Setup** button to see the format, page size, and header/footer options of the selected print style.

On the next page, we have shown the Page Setup dialogue box with the Header/Footer tab selected. Note the five icon buttons below the Footer text boxes, also shown here. These can be used to insert page number, total number of pages, date, time, and user's name, respectively, in both headers and footers. To do so, simply place the insertion cursor on one of the text boxes, then click the appropriate button.

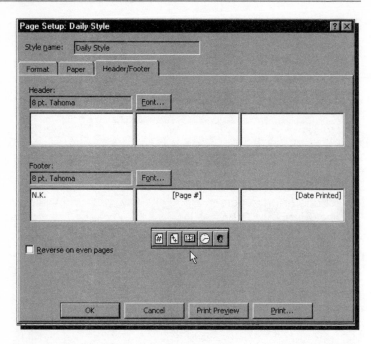

In the above footer set-up, we have inserted the user's initials in the left panel of the footer, the page number in the middle panel, and the date printed in the right panel. If you decide to show such information on your printout, it is entirely up to you where you choose to insert it. In addition, you can change the font type and font size of the information appearing on a header or footer.

If you want to change the font type and font size of the text appearing on the actual body of your printout, click the Format tab of the above dialogue box, and make appropriate selections under the displayed **Fonts** section. Pressing the **OK** button on the Page Setup dialogue box returns you to the Print dialogue box.

However, before committing anything to paper, use the **Pre<u>v</u>iew** button and save a few trees!

Planning a Meeting

Suppose we decide to invite other people into the meeting with the Managers on 8 July. First, locate the date of the meeting on the Calendar display and double-click the entry in question. In the displayed Assistant's 'Open Recurring Item' screen, click the 'Open this occurrence' radio button to display the Recurring Appointment dialogue box.

In this dialogue box, click the Attendee Availability tab to obtain the following screen, in which we typed the names of two colleagues we would like to be present at the meeting. If you had a Contacts list (see next section), you could also select one or more persons to attend this meeting by simply clicking the **Invite Others** button on the dialogue box below and selecting from the displayed list.

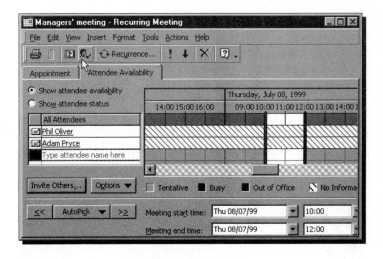

From here, you can organise meetings and send requests to participants and then track the status of their response provided, of course, you are connected to a local network. You can even give other Outlook users permissions to view your diary and to plan meetings with you at times when you are not so busy, but still be able to maintain private information in your diary.

Other Outlook Facilities

Apart from 'Calendar', the Outlook Shortcuts tab on the opening screen contains all the other elements needed to give you an effective time-management tool. These elements are accessed, as we have already seen, by appropriate icons situated on the left edge of the screen.

Contacts

The Contacts icon displays your contacts in a combined business card and list view. You can change the way information is displayed by using the **View, Current View** command. What is shown below is the Address Cards view format - you have the choice of six additional types of views.

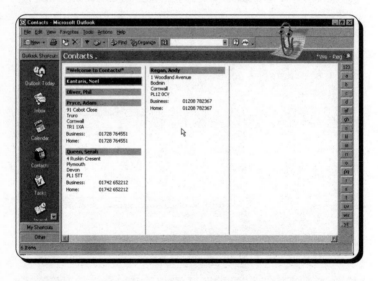

To add a new contact, click the **New** button, shown here, or to edit an existing entry, double-click on the contact name. Either action displays a multi-tab dialogue box, shown on the next page, in which you type relevant information. Contact lists can be saved under different group names, so that you can have one list for your friends, and another for your business.

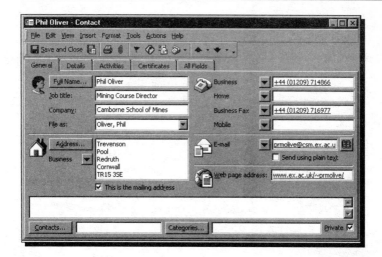

The task of filling in such detailed information about an individual might be daunting at first, but you will find it very useful later. For example, you only have to left click on the Web page address to be automatically connected to that Web page (of course, you will have to be connected to the Internet for that facility to work - see next chapter). Equally, you could click on the phone icon on the toolbar to display the AutoDialer, as shown below. Pressing the **Start Call** button connects you to your contact via the modem, provided you have a voice capable modem and a handset or microphone attached to it.

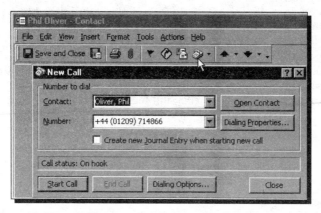

Tasks

Tasks appear in the daily and weekly views of Calendar, or can be displayed by clicking on the Task icon of the Outlook Options Bar. Tasks are used to organise your personal to-do list, as well as keep track of your business. Below we show a list of personal tasks, with their due date of completion.

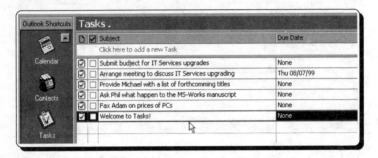

Tasks can be assigned to other people within your organisation, and can help you keep track of progress on work that other people do for you or in co-operation with you. For example, you might assign a task to a colleague, or a colleague might assign a task to you in a group effort.

A task assignment requires at least two people: one to send a task request and another to respond to it. When you send a task request, you give up ownership of the task, but can keep an updated copy of it in your task list and receive status reports, but you cannot change information in it. The person that receives the task request is the temporary owner of the task until acceptance of the task, in which case that person becomes the new, permanent owner of that task. Only temporary or permanent owners of a task can update that task. If a task is declined, ownership of the task is returned to the person who sent the task request.

To find out how to use the various functions appearing on a Tasks list, use the Help Assistant and search for 'tasks'. On the displayed list, click the Create a Task radio button to obtain the following screen.

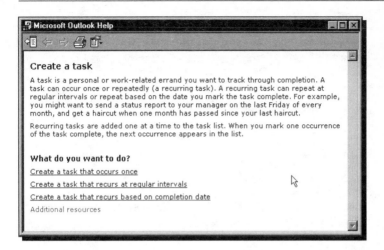

Look through the various topics listed, then go back to the

Assistant's displayed topics on 'Tasks', shown here, and work through all of them (there are an additional two relevant topics when you click the 'See more...' Option on the list).

Using Help in this way, you will learn quickly how to sort and give priority to tasks, track task progress, enter recurring tasks once, assign tasks to others, and keep complex task lists organised.

To add a new Task, click the **New** button, which displays a multi-tab dialogue box in which you type relevant information.

Journal

The following activities can be automatically recorded in Journal.

- E-mail messages
- Meeting requests
- Meeting responses
- Task requests
- Task responses

Clicking the Journal icon on the Outlook Options Bar, displays the following screen:

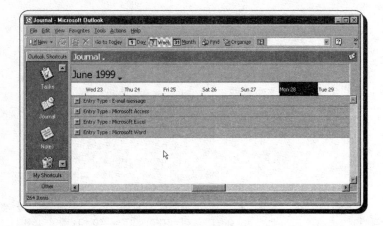

To find out how to use the various functions appearing on a Journal list, use the Help Assistant and search for 'Journal'. Go through all the displayed help options in a similar manner to that for Tasks. Try it, you will learn a lot.

3

E-mail with Outlook 2000

In what follows, it is assumed that your computer is capable of being connect to the Internet, or a local area network (LAN), so that you can receive e-mail. A connection to the Internet is usually made via a modem and a telephone line, an ethernet card to a LAN which itself is connected to the Internet, or an ISDN direct line. The latter provides faster connection, at present, but is more expensive than the alternatives. Finally, you may also need to find, and possibly subscribe to, a suitable Internet Service Provider (ISP) which is a company that allows you to connect to its Internet host.

There are many such providers in the UK. Most can be found in an Internet based PC magazine, your telephone directory, or possibly in adverts in the computer section of your newspaper. Be careful though before committing yourself to one provider as the quality of service and costs can vary considerably. One thing we can't do here is make specific recommendations, bur try and find someone who uses the company you decide on, or have a trial period with them.

All ISPs offer an e-mail address and mailbox facility to their customers; a mailbox being a storage area which holds your incoming messages until you connect to your ISP and download them to your computer so that you can read them. As long as your computer can access the Internet, you can use e-mail to keep in touch with friends and colleagues, anywhere in the world, provided they have their own e-mail address. The whole procedure of connecting to your ISP, downloading e-mail, filtering unwanted junk e-mail, saving and managing e-mail and other information, such as addresses of Web sites, can be done very easily in Outlook's Inbox - we will step you through the procedure later.

If you are using a modem to connect to the Internet, you must check that Windows is configured correctly for this type of communication medium. Usually, after connecting your modem and starting your computer, Windows will auto-detect its presence using its Plug and Play capability.

Next, you need to check that the correct driver (a small program that allows your computer to communicate with the modem) has been selected. To do this, click the Windows **Start** button and select **Settings, Control Panel** from the cascade menu, as shown below.

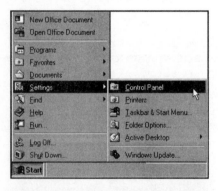

This displays various Control Panel options from which you should double-click the Modems icon, shown below, to start the relevant program.

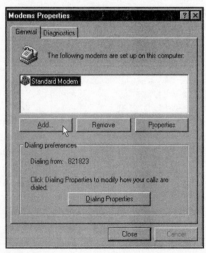

If in the Modems Properties dialogue box, shown to the left, the name of your actual modem is not displayed, then click the **Add** button to start the Install New Modem Wizard. Next, click the **Don't detect my modem; I will select it from a list** box, and press the **Next** button. Windows then searches your system and displays all the installed modem drivers.

If your modem's Manufacturer or Model does not appear on the displayed list, insert in your computer's appropriate drive the disc or CD that came with your modem and click the **Have Disk** button, as shown below.

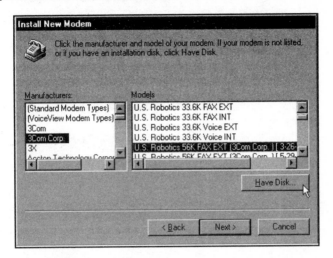

Finally, select the displayed modem driver and press the **OK** button to finish the installation.

The next step to be taken is to check that Windows has the correct communications set-up. To do this, click the Windows **Start** button and select **Settings, Control Panel** from the cascade menu, then double click the Network icon, shown here, which opens the Network dialogue box, part of which is shown at the top half on the next page. Make sure that all the displayed entries appear in that dialogue box (in our case these are under Windows 98 - under different versions of Windows the list could be slightly different). If you can see or suspect that some items are missing 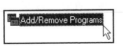 from the list, then double-click the Add/Remove Programs icon, shown here, to open its Properties dialogue box. In that box, click the Windows Setup tab and check that all the components under **Communications** are installed, as shown at the bottom half on the next page.

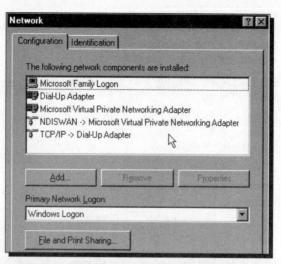

The Inbox Toolbar

You must have noticed by now that, apart from the symbols that appear on the screen of the various Outlook 2000 options, the icons on the Toolbar also change from one option to the other.

Below, we show the Inbox toolbar icons, before Outlook 2000 is configured for sending and receiving e-mail, with an explanation of their function.

 New Mail Message. Click the arrow to get ⇩

Print

Move to Folder

Delete

Reply

Reply to All

Find

Organise

Address Book

Office Assistant

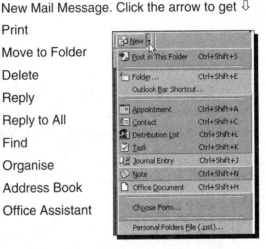

Left-clicking an icon button can display a drop-down menu, as shown above right, action a command, such as displaying the Folder List, or open an appropriate dialogue box so that you can, for example, access the address book or search for items, such as folders or files.

Note that when you first open a drop-down menu similar to the one shown above right, only the options on the darker bands are visible. However, a few seconds later, or when you place the mouse pointer on the down-arrow appearing at the bottom of the menu, the options on the lighter bands are also displayed. The latter are the less frequently used options, but once you select one, it joins the frequently used ones.

Configuring Outlook for E-mail

To configure Outlook 2000 to send and receive e-mail, use the **Tools**, **Options**, **Accounts** command to open the following dialogue box:

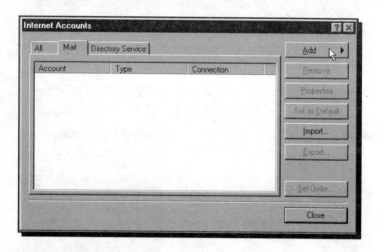

With the Mail tab pressed, click on the **Add** button and select **Mail** from the displayed menu to start the Internet Connection Wizard which asks you in successive screens to:

- Type in your name

- Type in your e-mail address. This is supplied to you by your ISP when you join their services.

- Specify the type of your incoming mail server, usually POP3, then type in the name of the 'Incoming' and 'Outgoing' mail server. This information is also supplied to you by your ISP.

- Type in your 'account name' and 'password' - again supplied to you by your ISP.

- Click the **Connect using my phone line** radio button (if that is how you are connected to the Internet), and select your ISP for your Dial-Up Networking connection.

If all is well, the final 'Congratulations' screen appears and
the Wizard places an additional **Send/Receive** button on the
Outlook's Inbox toolbar, as shown below.

You are now in a position to send and receive e-mail, but
before we do so, we need to add to the configuration so that
your e-mails show your signature. To do this, use the **Tools,
Options** command, and press the Mail Format tab of the
displayed dialogue box, as shown below.

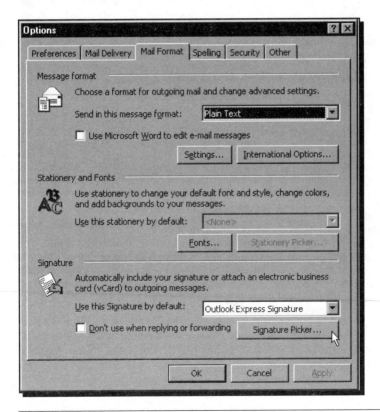

Next, click the **Signature Picker** button on the Options dialogue box, and click the **Edit** button on the displayed box. You can now type in what you want to appear at the bottom of each e-mail you send. This information for one of us is as shown below.

It is only polite to supply your name and e-mail address at the bottom of each electronic mail. In addition, you could create additional signatures which include your telephone number and/or your full address. In fact, you could create several signatures, each one with different content to be used depending on whether your e-mail is casual, formal, or professional, and switch between them as required.

As you can see from the Options dialogue box, shown on the previous page, Outlook 2000 supports many facilities relating to e-mail, including digital signatures. We suggest you spend some time looking at these before going on.

Sending and Receiving E-mail

Clicking the Inbox icon opens the screen below which will probably contain one or more messages from Microsoft. Note that the screen has two panes with the message titles appearing on the top pane. Clicking on a message highlights it and opens a Preview of it on the lower pane. Double-clicking on a message title opens the message in its own window.

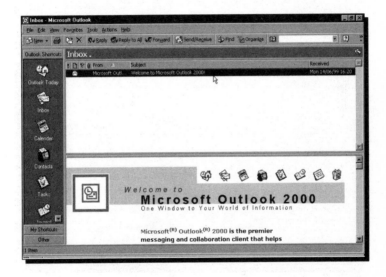

It is worth while reading these messages from Microsoft, as they demonstrate some of the features of Outlook 2000 and show how decorative your e-mail can be.

To check your mail, click the **Send/Receive** toolbar button which will download any new messages from your mailbox to your hard disc. You can then read and process your mail at your leisure without necessarily being still connected to the Internet. The default set-up of Outlook 2000 is such that after sending and receiving messages from your mail box, it automatically switches off your connection to your Internet Service Provider, to minimise telephone charges.

If, however, you have a permanent Internet connection, we suggest you make a change in the **Tools**, **Options**, **Mail Delivery** tab settings sheet, shown below. Selecting the **Check for new messages every** 10 **minutes** option will make the program check your mail box when it starts and at regular intervals while it is open.

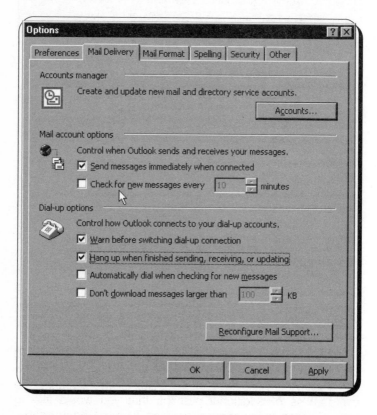

The best way to test out new e-mail features is to send a test message to your own e-mail address. This saves wasting somebody else's time, and the message can be very quickly checked to see the results. So, while we carry on with these tests, we suggest that you uncheck, for the moment, the **Hang up when finished sending, receiving, or updating** box and press the **Apply** and **OK** buttons.

Next, click the **New** button to open the New
Message dialogue box in which we compose a
short message, as shown below:

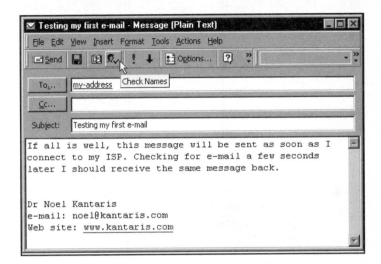

Note the address in the **To...** box is shown underlined. This
was automatically done by Outlook after typing in the text
string and clicking the Check Names icon on the toolbar,
because 'my-address' was associated with an e-mail address
in the Address Book and Outlook picked it up. We could, of
course, have typed the full e-mail address in the **To...** box,
but the above method is a much easier and neater way.

Each e-mail should have a short **Subject** which is what will
appear on the upper Inbox panel when the message is
received by the recipient. The **Cc...** Box is where you include
the address of additional persons that you would like to
receive the same message. To send the message,
simply press the **Send** button which causes the
New Message box to close down. What has
happened here is that the message has been placed in
Outlook's Outbox, waiting for you to perhaps compose
another e-mail. To see that your message is waiting in the
Outbox, click the **Inbox** button, shown here, which
opens up a list of folders, as shown overleaf.

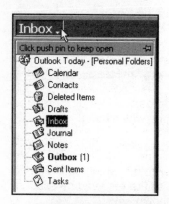

As you can see, the Outbox folder is marked with one (1) item. Should you want to edit a message in the Outbox, double-click its folder which opens an Outbox window listing all the messages held in it. Double-clicking one of these, opens the selected message ready for you to edit, as shown below.

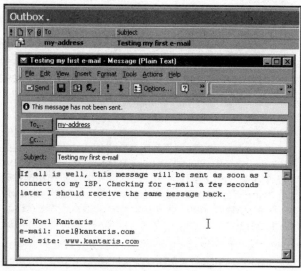

Having edited a message, click the **Send** button again to again place it in the Outbox.

To send a message, click the **Send/Receive** button and follow the connection procedure to your ISP. Verification of what is happening is displayed at 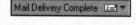 the bottom right corner of Outlook's screen.

Now, clicking on the **Sent Items** button reveals that the Outbox folder is empty, but there is a message waiting for us in the Inbox folder. This is the very message we sent a few seconds earlier which came back to us at the speed of light, well almost!

To see the received message, double-click the Inbox folder which opens it and lists all the received messages, as shown below.

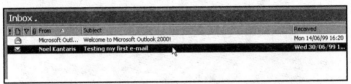

Highlighting a message displays its contents on the lower pane of the Inbox screen, while double-clicking it, opens the message in its own window. Looking at messages without opening them, can be used to transfer them to preselected folders, using the **Move to Folder** toolbar button; you could, for example, have a folder for each of the most important persons in your private or business life, thus keeping their messages together.

If you have received a message that you don't want to keep, then highlight it and press the **Delete** toolbar button. Deleted items are held in a folder,

 in case you want to resurrect them. To empty this folder, click the **Deleted Items** button on the Outlook Shortcuts menu bar to reveal all the items held in this folder. To permanently delete an item, left-click it to select it, then either press the **Delete** button or the **Del** keyboard key. You will be asked to confirm deletion before the action is carried out.

Formatting your E-mail

Apart from sending messages in Plain Text, Outlook 2000, allows you to format your e-mail in Microsoft Outlook Rich Text, or HTML (the HyperText Markup Language used to format most documents on the Web). To select one of these, use the **Tools, Options** command to open the dialogue box below.

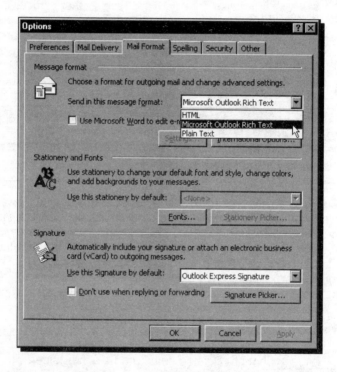

You can also select in the above dialogue box whether to use Microsoft Word as your default e-mail editor. Any of the above mentioned formats can be used with either Outlook or Word as your e-mail editor. Furthermore, you can use the **Actions**, **New Mail Message Using** command to create a single message in a format, or e-mail editor, other than the defaults that you have selected by choosing the message format or e-mail editor from the displayed menu.

To show you what you can do with the Microsoft Outlook Rich Text format, we have prepared below a short message using several text enhancements (see Chapter 6 for details).

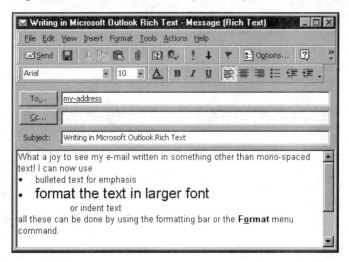

However, remember that not everyone will be able to read the work you spent ages creating. Below we show what someone who does not have such an enhanced e-mail program will receive.

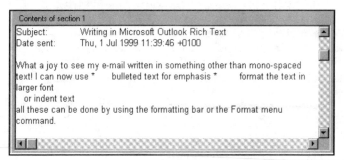

As you can see, all tabulation and text enhancements have been lost. Therefore, if you use Outlook's Rich Text format avoid excessive text enhancements. The same can be said for Outlook's pre-formatted stationery under the HTML option.

Using E-mail Attachments

Sometimes, when you receive an e-mail with Outlook 2000, you might find at the bottom of the main text area, a file displayed, as follows:

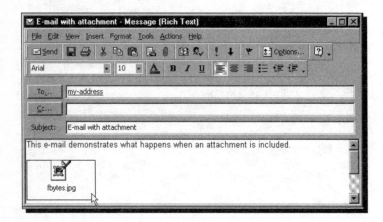

This indicates an attachment to the e-mail which can be a drawing, another formatted document, a photo, or even a sound and video file.

Until fairly recently, e-mail on the Internet was good only for short text notes. You could not send attachments like the ones mentioned above. That has now changed with the advent of MIME, which stands for Multipurpose Internet Mail Extension. With Outlook 2000 you can even send your favourite Web page as an attachment to an e-mail.

To view or save an attachment file, double-click its icon. Such files can also be saved with the **File**, **Save Attachments** command, or by right-clicking it and selecting the **Save As** option from the displayed context menu.

Adding Attachments to your E-mail

If you want to include an attachment to your main e-mail message, you simply click the **Insert file** toolbar button and select the file to attach. This opens the Insert File dialogue box, for you to select the file, or files, you want to go with your message.

Before you start sending attachments with your e-mail, make sure that the person you are sending your message to has e-mail software capable of decoding them. In our experience most people seem to stick to their tried and trusted 'old' software that does not. If that is the case, only include one attachment per e-mail and mention in the text area of your e-mail what software you used to create the attachment; it will help the recipient to decipher it.

In Outlook 2000 the attached files are 'placed' at the bottom of your message, as shown below, each with a distinctive icon that tells the recipient what the file is. Double-clicking such an icon will open the file in its application, provided the person receiving your e-mail has the relevant application. Again, it is only polite to include a short description of what the applications are, as shown below.

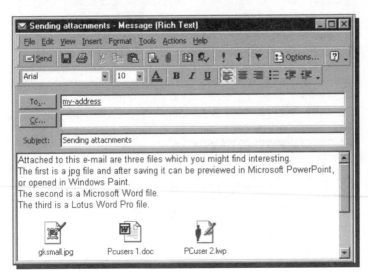

Viewing and Sending Web Pages

You can use Outlook 2000 to view Web pages by clicking sites listed under the **Favorites** menu command, or create shortcuts to Web pages that you visit frequently and add them to the list.

Even more interesting is the ease with which you can send a Web page as an e-mail. We will demonstrate the process by left-clicking one entry from our **Favorites** list which connects us to the Internet and displays the relevant Web page, as shown below.

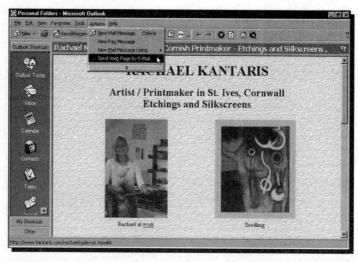

Next, click the **Actions** menu command and select the **Send Web Page by E-Mail** option from the drop-down menu, as shown above, which causes a New Mail Message screen to open for you to type the recipient's address. In the main body of the e-mail Outlook automatically includes the attachment icon shown to the left, below which you can add your text.

To preview such a file, click the paper clip file attachment icon in the preview pane header, select and click the filename.

Spell Checking

Many of the e-mail messages we receive are full of errors and spelling mistakes. Some people do not seem to read their work before clicking the **Send** button. With Outlook 2000 this could be avoided, as the program is linked to the spell checker that comes with Microsoft's Office. To try it out, prepare a message in the New Message window, but make an obvious spelling mistake, maybe like ours below. Pressing the **F7** function key, or using the **Tools**, **Spelling** command, will start the process.

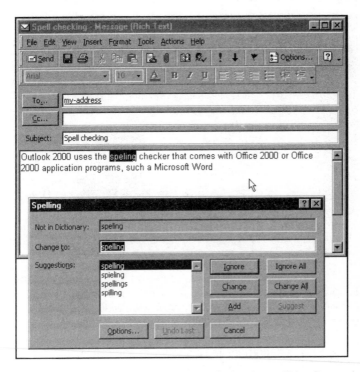

Any words not recognised by the spell checker will be flagged up as above. If you are happy with the word just click one of the **Ignore** buttons, if not, you can type a correction in the **Change to** field, or accept one of the **Suggestions**, and then click the **Change** button.

Selecting Options Settings

Now that we have finished experimenting with sending and receiving e-mail, it is a good idea to make some permanent changes to Outlook's settings. Use the **Tools, Options** command to open the Options dialogue box.

We suggest you make the following options selections:

• Click the Spelling tab and select the **Always check spelling before sending** option, so that every message you write is checked before it is sent.

• Click the Mail Delivery tab and select **Hang up when finished sending, receiving, or updating** option, so that you don't forget to disconnect your phone.

• Click the Preferences tab and click the **E-mail Options** button. In the **When replying to a message** box you can select to include or not include the original message with your reply. If you choose to include it, make sure you edit it first - it is pointless making your reply longer by including the whole of the original message. If, on the other hand, you choose not to include it, make sure you refer to the points made in it; don't just answer 'yes' or 'no'.

• Click the Other tab and check the **Empty the Deleted Items folder upon exiting** box.

Obviously there are a lot more selections you could make, but we leave these to you. Very soon, after you have been using Outlook 2000 for a while, you will know yourself what options and preferences to choose.

* * *

Outlook has many more features, far too numerous to discuss in the space allocated in this book. What we have tried to do, is give you enough basic information so that you can have the confidence to explore the rest of Outlook's capabilities by yourself.

4

Microsoft Word Basics

Word is started in Windows either by clicking the **Start** button

then selecting **Programs** and clicking on the 'Microsoft Word' icon on the cascade menu, clicking the Word icon, or the 'Open Office Document' icon on the Office Shortcut Bar, or by clicking and double-clicking on a Word document file. In the latter case the document will be loaded into Word at the same time.

If you have used a previous version of Word it might be a good idea to use **The Office Assistant** and search for *what's new*. Selecting the 'What's new in Microsoft Word 2000?' option (pointed to below), displays a further list of options which you might like to view.

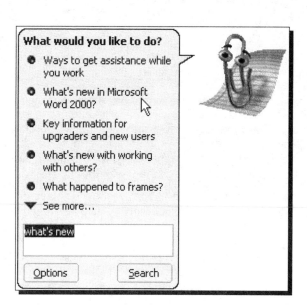

The Word Screen

The opening 'blank' screen of Word 2000 is shown below. It is perhaps worth spending some time looking at the various parts that make up this screen. Word follows the usual Microsoft Windows conventions and if you are familiar with these you can skip through this section. Otherwise a few minutes might be well spent here.

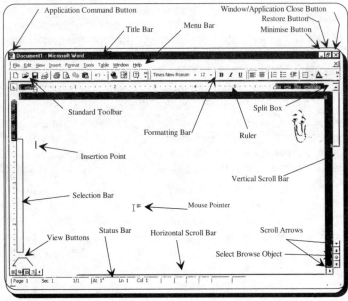

The window as shown takes up the full screen area available. If you click on the application restore button, you can make Word show in a smaller window. This can be useful when you are running several applications at the same time and you want to transfer between them with the mouse.

Note that in this case, the Word window displays an empty document with the title 'Document1', and has a solid 'Title bar', indicating that it is the active application window. Although multiple windows can be displayed simultaneously, you can only enter data into the active window (which will always be displayed on top). Title bars of non active windows appear a lighter shade than that of the active one.

The Word screen is divided into several areas which have the following functions:

Area

Function

Command buttons

Clicking on the command button, (see upper-left corner of the Word window), displays a pull-down menu which can be used to control the program window. It allows you to restore, move, size, minimise, maximise, and close the window.

Title Bar

The bar at the top of a window which displays the application name and the name of the current document.

Minimise Button

When clicked on, this button minimises a document to an icon, or the application to the Windows Taskbar.

Restore Button

When clicked on, this button restores the active window to the position and size that was occupied before it was maximised. The restore button is then replaced by a Maximise button, as shown here, which is used to set the window to full screen size.

Close button

The extreme top right button that you click to close a window.

Menu Bar

The bar below the Title bar which allows you to choose from several menu options.

Clicking on a menu item displays the pull-down menu associated with that item.

Standard Toolbar

The bar below the Menu bar which contains buttons that give you mouse click access to the functions most often used in the program. These are grouped according to function.

Formatting Bar

The buttons on the Formatting Bar allow you to change the attributes of a font, such as italic and underline, and also to format text in various ways. The Formatting Bar contains three boxes; a style box, a font box and a size box which show which style, font and size of characters are currently being used. These boxes give access to other installed styles, fonts and character sizes.

Ruler

The area where you can see and set tabulation points and indents.

Split Box

The area above the top vertical scroll button which when dragged allows you to split the screen.

Scroll Bars

The areas on the screen that contain scroll boxes in vertical and horizontal bars. Clicking on these bars allows you to control the part of a document which is visible on the screen.

Scroll Arrows

The arrowheads at each end of each scroll bar at which you can click to scroll the screen up and down one line, or left and right 10% of the screen, at a time.

Selection Bar	The area on the screen in the left margin of the Word window (marked here with a box for convenience), where the mouse pointer changes to an arrow that slants to the right. Clicking the left mouse button once selects the current line, while clicking twice selects the current paragraph.
Insertion pointer	The pointer used to specify the place of text insertion.
Views Buttons	Clicking these buttons changes screen views quickly.
Status Bar	The bottom line of the document window that displays status information.

The Standard Toolbar

This is located below the Menu bar at the top of the Word screen and contains command buttons. To action a command, left-click its button with the mouse. Not only can you control what buttons show on the various toolbars, but as you work with Word the buttons you use most often are displayed on them automatically.

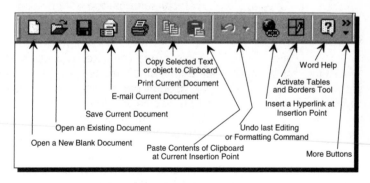

The use of these Standard Toolbar buttons will be discussed in great detail, with worked examples, in the next chapter.

The Formatting Bar

This is located to the right of or below the Standard Toolbar, and is divided into sections that contain command buttons, as shown below.

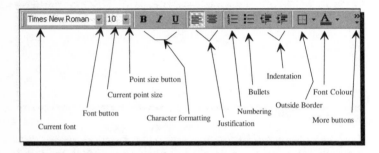

The Current font box shows the current typeface. Clicking on the down-arrow button to the right of it allows you to change the typeface of any selected text. The Current point size box shows the size of selected characters which can be changed by clicking on the down-arrow button next to it and selecting another size from the displayed list.

Next, are three character formatting buttons which allow you to enhance selected text by emboldening, italicising, or underlining it. The next two buttons allow you to change the justification of a selected paragraph, and the next four help you set the different types of Numbering and Indentation options. The last two buttons allow you to add an Outside Border to selected text or objects, and change the font colour of selected text.

Clicking on the More Buttons area, opens up the menu shown here with additional options for justifying selected paragraphs and highlighting text. The first option displays the name of the current style (Normal) in a box. Clicking the down-arrow against this box, opens up a menu of default paragraph styles with their font sizes.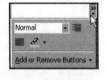
Once the Style box is opened, from then on, it appears to the left of the Font box, replacing other formatting icons.

The Status Bar

This is located at the bottom of the Word window and is used to display statistics about the active document.

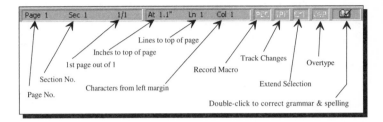

For example, when a document is being opened, the Status bar displays for a short time its name and length in terms of total number of characters. Once a document is opened, the Status bar displays the statistics of the document at the insertion point; here it is on Page 1, Section 1, 1 character from the left margin.

Double-clicking the left of the status bar displays the Find and Replace dialogue box, as shown below.

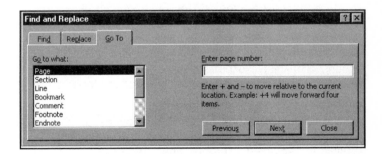

This is shown with the **Go To** tab selected. You can choose which page, section line, etc., of the document to go to, or you can use the other tabs to **Find** and **Replace** text (more about this later).

Double-clicking the other features on the Status bar will activate these features.

Creating Word Documents

When the program is first used, all Word's features default to those shown on page 68 (apart from showing the ruler). It is quite possible to use Word in this mode, without changing any main settings, but obviously it is possible to customise the package to your needs, as we shall see later.

Entering Text

In order to illustrate some of Word's capabilities, you need to have a short text at hand. We suggest you type the memo displayed below into a new document. At this stage, don't worry if the length of the lines below differ from those on your display.

As you type in text, any time you want to force a new line, or paragraph, just press <Enter>. While typing within a paragraph, Word sorts out line lengths automatically (known as 'word wrap'), without you having to press any keys to move to a new line. If you make a mistake while typing, press the <BkSp> key enough times to erase the mistake and start again.

MEMO TO PC USERS

Networked Computers

The microcomputers in the Data Processing room are a mixture of IBM compatible PCs with Pentium processors running at various speeds. They all have 3.5" floppy drives of 1.44MB capacity, and most also have CD-ROM drives. The PCs are connected to various printers via a network; the Laser printers available giving best output.

The computer you are using will have at least a 3.0GB capacity hard disc on which a number of software programs, including the latest version of Windows, have been installed. To make life easier, the hard disc is highly structured with each program installed in a separate folder (directory).

Moving Around a Document

You can move the cursor around a document with the normal direction keys, and with the key combinations listed below.

To move	*Press*
Left one character	←
Right one character	→
Up one line	↑
Down one line	↓
Left one word	Ctrl+←
Right one word	Ctrl+→
To beginning of line	Home
To end of line	End
To paragraph beginning	Ctrl+↑
To paragraph end	Ctrl+↓
Up one screen	PgUp
Down one screen	PgDn
To top of previous page	Ctrl+PgUp
To top of next page	Ctrl+PgDn
To beginning of file	Ctrl+Home
To end of file	Ctrl+End

To jump to a specified page number in a multi-page document, either double-click the left of the status bar to display the Find and Replace dialogue box, then click the Go To tab, or use the **Edit**, **Go To** command (or <Ctrl+G>), shown here and to be explained shortly.

Obviously, you need to become familiar with the above methods of moving the cursor around a document, particularly if you are not using a mouse and you spot an error in a document which needs to be corrected, which is the subject of the latter half of this chapter.

Templates and Paragraph Styles

As we saw under the Formatting Bar section earlier, when you start Word for the first time, the Style box contains the word **Normal**. This means that all the text you have entered, at the moment, is shown in the Normal paragraph style which is one of the styles available in the NORMAL template. Every document produced by Word has to use a template, and NORMAL is the default. A template contains, both the document page settings and a set of formatting instructions which can be applied to text.

Changing Paragraph Styles

To change the style of a paragraph, do the following:

- Place the cursor (insertion pointer) on the paragraph in question, say the title line

- Left click the Style Status button, and select the **Heading 1** style.

The selected paragraph reformats instantly in bold, and in Arial typeface of point size 16.

With the cursor in the second line of text, select **Heading 3** which reformats the line in Arial 13. Your memo should now look presentable, as shown below.

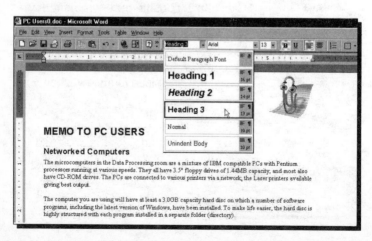

Document Screen Displays

Word provides four display views, Normal, Web Layout, Print Layout, and Outline, as well as the options to view your documents in a whole range of screen enlargements by selecting **Zoom**. You control all these viewing options with the **View** sub-menu, shown here, and when a document is displayed you can switch freely between them. When first loaded the screen displays in Print Layout view.

The view options have the following effect, and can also be accessed by clicking the View buttons on the left of the Status bar.

Normal Layout

A view that simplifies the layout of the page so that you can type, edit and format text quickly. In normal view, page boundaries, headers and footers, backgrounds, drawing objects, and pictures that do not have the '**In line with text**' wrapping style do not appear.

Web Layout

A view that optimises the layout of a document to make online reading easier. Use this layout view when you are creating a Web page or a document that is viewed on the screen. In Web layout view, you can see backgrounds, text is wrapped to fit the window, and graphics are positioned just as they are in a Web browser.

Print Layout

Provides a WYSIWYG (what you see is what you get) view of a document. The text displays in the typefaces and point sizes you specify, and with the selected attributes.

This view is useful for editing headers and footers, for adjusting margins, and for working with columns and drawing objects. All text boxes or frames, tables, graphics, headers, footers, and footnotes appear on the screen as they will in the final printout.

Outline Layout

Provides a collapsible view of a document, which enables you to see its organisation at a glance. You can display all the text in a file, or just the text that uses the paragraph styles you specify. Using this mode, allows you to quickly rearrange large sections of text. Some people like to create an outline of their document first, consisting of all the headings, then to sort out the document structure and finally fill in the text.

With large documents, you can create what is known as a *Master* document by starting with an Outline View, and then designate headings in the outline as sub-documents. When you save the master document, Word assigns names to each sub-document based on the text you use in the outline headings. You can also convert an existing document to a master document and then divide it into sub-documents, or you can add existing documents to a master document to make them sub-documents.

In a master document, you can quickly change the top-level structure of the document by adding, removing, combining, splitting, renaming, and rearranging sub-documents. You can also create a table of contents, index, cross-references, and headers and footers for all of the sub-documents. The master document's template applies to all the sub-documents, so the entire document has a consistent design. Printing a master document is a fast way to print all the sub-documents without opening them individually. A Master document can be thought of as a 'container for a set of separate files or sub-documents.

Full Screen

Selecting the **View, Full Screen** command, displays a clean, uncluttered screen; the Toolbars, Ruler, Scroll bars, and Status bar are removed. To return to the usual screen, click the **Close Full Screen** button on the icon which appears at the bottom of your screen when in this mode.

Zoom

Selecting the **View, Zoom** command, displays the Zoom dialogue box (we only show the left side of it here), in which you can change the viewing magnification factor from its default value of 100%.

Changing Default Options

Modifying Margins

To change the standard page margins for your entire document from the cursor position onward, or for selected text (more about this later), do the following:

- Select the **File, Page Setup** command
- Click the left mouse button at the **Margins** tab on the displayed dialogue box, shown below.

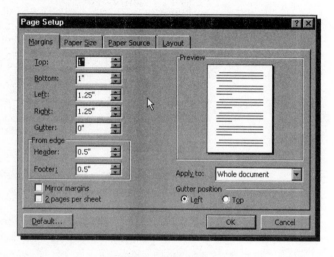

The 'Preview' page to the right of the box shows how your changes will look on a real page.

Changing the Default Paper Size

To change the default paper size from the size set during installation to a different size, do the following:

- Select the **File, Page Setup** command
- Click the left mouse button at the **Paper Size** tab on the displayed dialogue box

- Click the down-arrow against the **Paper Size** box to reveal the list of available paper sizes

- Change the page size to your new choice, and press the **Default** button and confirm that you wish this change to affect all new documents based on the Normal template.

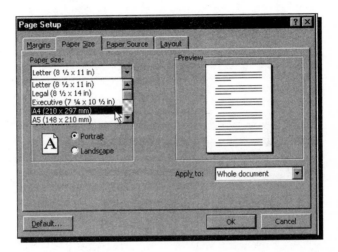

Check that the paper size matches that in your printer, otherwise you may get strange results. The orientation of the printed page is normally **Portrait** (text prints across the page width), but you could choose to change this to **Landscape** which prints across the page length, as long as your printer can print in landscape.

All changes you can make to your document from the Page Setup dialogue box can be applied to either the whole document or to the rest of the document starting from the current position of the insertion pointer. To carry out such changes click the down-arrow button against the **Apply to** box and choose appropriately from the drop-down menu list.

Modifying the Paper Source

Clicking on the third Page Setup tab, displays yet another

dialogue box, part of which is shown here, from which you can select the paper source. You might have a printer that holds paper in trays, in which case you might want to specify that the first page (headed paper perhaps), should be taken from one tray, while the rest of the paper should be taken from a different tray.

Modifying the Page Layout

Clicking the last Page Setup tab displays the Layout box, part

of which is shown here. From this dialogue box you can set options for headers and footers, section breaks, vertical alignment and whether to add line numbers or borders.

The default for **Section Start** is 'New Page' which allows the section to start at the top of the next page. Pressing the down arrow against this option, allows you to change this choice.

In the Headers and Footers section of the dialogue box, you can specify whether you want one header or footer for even-numbered pages and a different header or footer for odd-numbered pages. You can further specify if you want a different header or footer on the first page from the header or footer used for the rest of the document. Word can align the top line with the 'Top' margin, but this can be changed with the **Vertical Alignment** option.

Changing Other Default Options

You can also change the default options available to you in Word 2000, by selecting the **Tools, Options** command. Using the displayed Options dialogue box below, you can, amongst other things, do the following:

* Specify the default **View** options. For example, you can select whether non-printing formatting characters, such as Tabs, Spaces, and Paragraph marks, are shown or not.

* Adjust the **General** Word settings, such as background re-pagination, display of the recently used file-list, and selection of units of measurement.

* Adjust the **Print** settings, such as allowing background printing, reverse print order, or choose to print comments with documents.

* Change the **Save** options, such as selecting to always create a backup copy of your work.

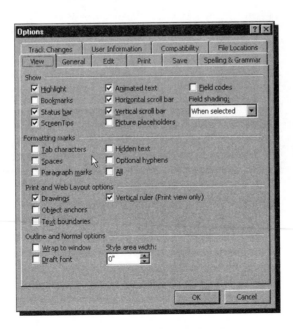

Saving to a File

To save a document to disc, use either of the commands:

- **File, Save** (or click the Save toolbar icon) which is used when a document has previously been saved to disc in a named file; using this command saves your work under the existing filename automatically without prompting you.

- **File, Save As** command which is used when you want to save your document with a different name from the one you gave it already.

Using the **File, Save As** command (or the very first time you use the **File, Save** command when a document has no name), opens the following dialogue box:

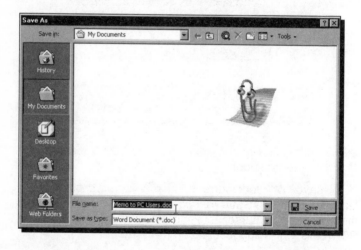

Note that the first 255 characters of the first paragraph of a new document is highlighted in the **File name** field box and the program is waiting for you to type a new name. Any name you type (less than 255 characters) will replace the existing name. Filenames cannot include any of the following keyboard characters: /, \, >, <, *, ?, ", |, :, or ;. Word adds the file extension **.doc** automatically and uses it to identify its documents.

You can select a drive other than the one displayed, by clicking the down arrow against the **Save in** text box at the top of the Save As dialogue box. You can also select a folder in which to save your work. If you do not have a suitably named folder, then you can create one using the Create New Folder button on the Save As dialogue box, shown below.

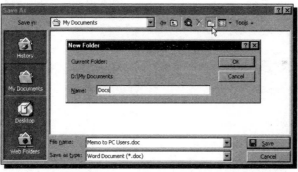

We used this facility to create a folder called **Docs** within the **My Documents** folder.

To save our work currently in memory, we selected the **Docs** folder in the **Save in** field of the Save As dialogue box, then moved the cursor into the **File name** box, and typed **PC Users 1**. We suggest you do the same.

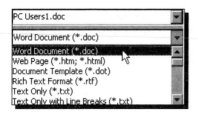

By clicking the **Save as type** button at the bottom of the Save As dialogue box, you can save the Document Template, or the Text Only parts of your work, or you can save your document in a variety of other formats, including Rich Text, and Web Page (HTML).

Selecting File Location

You can select where Word is to look automatically for your document files when you first choose to open or save a document by selecting the **Tools**, **Options** command, click the File Locations tab of the displayed Options dialogue box, and modifying the location of the document files, as shown below.

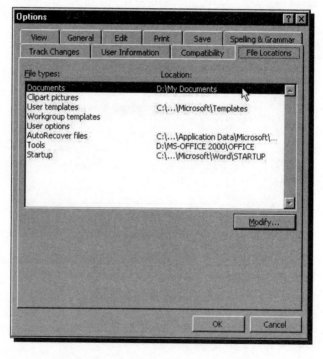

As you can see, the default location of other types of files is also given in the above dialogue box.

Microsoft suggests that you store documents, worksheets, presentations, databases, and other files you are currently working on, in the **My Documents** folder. This, of course, is a matter of preference, so we leave it to you to decide. We prefer to create sub-folders within the **My Documents** folder and save files from the same application in one sub-folder.

Document Properties

A useful feature in Word is the facility to add document properties to every file by selecting the **File, Properties** command. A Properties box, as shown below, opens for you to type additional information about your document.

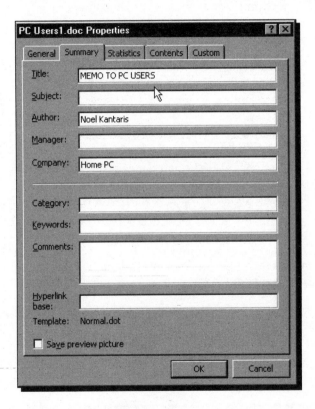

In this box you can select to add a manager, company, or category name to group files together for ease of retrieval.

To do this on a more regular basis, make sure that the **Prompt for Document Properties** box in the Save Options dialogue box (use the **Tools, Options** command and click the Save tab of the Options dialogue box) is selected and appears ticked.

Closing a Document

There are several ways to close a document in Word. Once you have saved it you can click its 'X' close button, or double-click on the Document Control button at the left end of the menu bar; you would usually use these when you have several files open together.

If you want to close the current document, and then open a new one or a different one, do the following:

* Choose **File, Close** to close the current document (remove it from your computer's memory) before using either

* **File, New** (or clicking ) to create a new file, or

* **File, Open** (or clicking) to use an existing file.

If the document (or file) has changed since the last time it was saved, you will be given the option to save it before it is removed from memory.

If a document is not closed before a new document is opened, then both documents will be held in memory, but only one will be the current document. To find out which documents are held in memory, use the Taskbar, or the **Window** command to reveal the following menu options:

In this case, the third document in the list is the current document, and to make another document the current one, either type the document number, or point at its name and click the left mouse button.

To close a document which is not the current document, use the **Window** command, make it current, and close it with one of the above methods.

5

Editing Word Documents

It will not be long, when using Word, before you will need to edit your document. One of the first things you will notice is that misspelled words are unobtrusively underlined in a red wavy line and that ungrammatical phrases are similarly underlined in green. To demonstrate this facility, use the **File, New** command (or click 🗋) to create a new file, and type the words 'Computors are fun to usr', exactly as misspelled here. What should appear on your screen is shown below, but with the misspelled words underlined in a red wavy line.

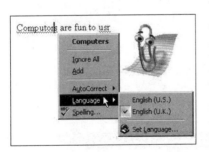

Right-clicking the first word allows you to correct it, as shown here. To correct such a word, left-click on 'Computers'. You even have a choice of English. Next, place the cursor on 'usr' and right-click once more to display:

This is possibly the most timesaving enhancement in editing misspelled words as you type. The spell and grammar checker will be discussed later in more detail.

Other editing could include deleting unwanted words or adding extra text in the document. All these operations are very easy to carry out. For small deletions, such as letters or words, the easiest method to adopt is the use of the <Del> or <BkSp> keys.

With the <Del> key, position the cursor on the left of the first letter you want to delete and press <Del>. With the <BkSp> key, position the cursor immediately to the right of the character to be deleted and press <BkSp>. In both cases the rest of the line moves to the left to take up the space created by the deleting process.

Word processing is usually carried out in the insert mode. Any characters typed will be inserted at the cursor location (insertion point) and the following text will be pushed to the right, and down, to make room. To insert blank lines in your text, place the cursor at the beginning of the line where the blank line is needed and press <Enter>. To remove the blank line, position the cursor on it and press <Del>.

When larger scale editing is needed you have several alternatives. You could first 'select' the text to be altered, then use the **Cut, Copy** and **Paste** operations available in the **Edit** sub-menu, or click on the Toolbar button alternatives shown here.

Another method of copying or moving text is to use the 'drag and drop' facility which requires you to highlight a word, grab it with the left mouse button depressed, and drop it in the required place in your text. This facility will also be discussed shortly in some detail.

Adding Buttons to the Standard Toolbar

When you first use Word, the **Cut** button shown above is not on the default Standard Toolbar. To place it there, first click the **More Buttons** icon, then the **Add or Remove Buttons**,

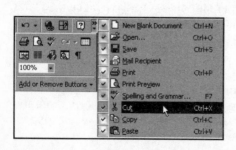

and from the displayed menu select the one required, as shown to the left. From then on, the selected button appears on the Toolbar, but may displace other buttons.

Selecting Text

The procedure in Word, as with most Windows based applications, is first to select the text to be altered before any operation, such as formatting or editing, can be carried out on it. Selected text is highlighted on the screen. This can be carried out in two main ways:

A. Using the keyboard, to select:

• A block of text.	Position the cursor on the first character to be selected and hold down the <Shift> key while using the arrow keys to highlight the required text, then release the <Shift> key.
• From the present position to the end of the line.	Use <Shift+End>.
• From the present cursor position to the beginning of the line.	Use <Shift+Home>.
• From the present cursor position to the end of the document.	Use <Shift+Ctrl+End>.
• From the present cursor position to the beginning of the document.	Use <Shift+Ctrl+Home>.

B. With the mouse, to select:

- A block of text.

  Press down the left mouse button at the beginning of the block and while holding it pressed, drag the cursor across the block so that the desired text is highlighted, then release the mouse button.

- A word.

  Double-click within the word.

- A line.

  Place the mouse pointer on the selection bar, just to the left of the line, and click once (for multiple lines, after selecting the first line, drag the pointer in the selection bar).

- A sentence.

  Hold the <Ctrl> key down and click in the sentence.

- A paragraph.

  Place the mouse pointer in the selection bar and double-click (for multiple paragraphs, after selecting the first paragraph, drag the pointer in the selection bar) or triple-click in the paragraph.

- The whole document.

  Place the mouse pointer in the selection bar, hold the <Ctrl> key down and click once.

Copying Blocks of Text

Once text has been selected it can be copied to another
location in your present document, to another Word
document, or to another Windows application, via the
clipboard. As with most of the editing and formatting
operations there are several alternative ways of doing this, as
follows:

• Use the **Edit, Copy** command sequence from the
  menu, to copy the selected text to the Windows
  clipboard, moving the cursor to the start of where you
  want the copied text to be placed, and using the **Edit,
  Paste** command.

• Use the quick key combinations, <Ctrl+Ins> (or
  <Ctrl+C>) to copy and <Shift+Ins> (or <Ctrl+V>) to
  paste, once the text to be copied has been selected.
  This does not require the menu bar to be activated.

• Use the 'Copy to clipboard' and 'Paste from clipboard'
  Standard Toolbar buttons; you can of course only use
  this method with a mouse.

To copy the same text again to another
location, or to any open document window or
application, move the cursor to the new
location and paste it there with any of these
methods. It is stored on the clipboard until it
is replaced by the next Cut, or Copy
operation.

• Selected text can be copied by holding the <Ctrl> key

depressed while dragging the mouse with
the left button held down. The drag pointer
is an arrow with an attached square - the
vertical dotted line showing the point of
insertion. The new text will insert itself where placed,
even if the overstrike mode is in operation. Text copied
by this method is not placed on the clipboard, so
multiple copies are not possible as with other methods.

Moving Blocks of Text

Selected text can be moved to any location in the same document by either of the following:

- Using the **Edit, Cut,** command or <Shift+Del> (or <Ctrl+X>).

- Clicking the 'Cut to clipboard' Standard Toolbar button, shown here.

Next, move the cursor to the required new location and use either of the following procedures:

- The **Edit, Paste** command.

- Any other paste actions as described previously.

The moved text will be placed at the cursor location and will force any existing text to make room for it. This operation can be cancelled by simply pressing <Esc>. Once moved, multiple copies of the same text can be produced by other **Paste** operations.

   Selected text can be moved by dragging the mouse with the left button held down. The drag pointer is an arrow with an attached square - the vertical dotted line showing the point of insertion.

Deleting Blocks of Text

When text is 'cut' it is removed from the document, but placed on the clipboard until further text is either copied or cut. With Word any selected text can be deleted by pressing **Edit, Cut,** or clicking the 'Cut to Clipboard' Standard Toolbar icon, shown here, or by pressing the <Del>, or <BkSp> keys. However, using **Edit, Cut,** allows you to use the **Edit, Paste** command, but using the <Del> or <BkSp> keys, does not.

The Undo Command

As text is lost with the delete command, you should use it with caution, but if you do make a mistake all is not lost as long as you act promptly. The **Edit, Undo** command or <Ctrl+Z> (or <Alt+BkSp>) reverses your most recent editing or formatting commands.

You can also use the Undo Standard Toolbar button, shown here, to undo one of several editing or formatting mistakes (press the down arrow to the right of the button to see a list of your recent changes, as shown here).

Undo does not reverse any action once editing changes have been saved to file. Only editing done since the last save can be reversed.

Finding and Changing Text

Word allows you to search for specifically selected text, or character combinations. To do this use the **Find** or the **Replace** option from the **Edit** command sub-menu.

Using the **Find** option (<Ctrl+F>), will highlight each occurrence of the supplied text in turn so that you can carry out some action on it, such as change its font or appearance.

Using the **Replace** option (<Ctrl+H>), allows you to specify what replacement is to be automatically carried out. For example, in a long article you may decide to replace every occurrence of the word 'microcomputers' with the word 'PCs'.

To illustrate the **Replace** procedure, either select the option from the **Edit** sub-menu or use the quick key combination <Ctrl+H>. This opens the Find and Replace dialogue box shown on the next page.

Clicking the **More** button displays the top half of the composite screen dump shown below.

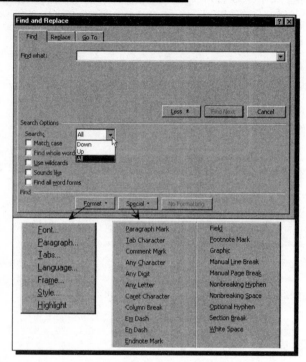

Towards the bottom of the dialogue box, there are five check boxes; the first two can be used to match the case of letters in the search string, and/or a whole word, while the last three can be used for wildcard, 'sounds like' or 'word forms' matching.

The two buttons, **Format** and **Special**, situated at the bottom of the dialogue box, let you control how the search is carried out. The lists of available options, when either of these buttons is pressed, are displayed above. You will of course only see one or the other, but not both as shown here.

You can force both the search and the replace operations to work with exact text attributes. For example, selecting:

* The **<u>F</u>ont** option from the list under **F<u>o</u>rmat**, displays a dialogue box in which you select a font (such as Arial, Times New Roman, etc.); a font-style (such as regular, bold, italic, etc.); an underline option (such as single, double, etc.); and special effects (such as strike-through, superscript, subscript, etc.).

* The **<u>P</u>aragraph** option, lets you control indentation, spacing (before and after), and alignment.

* The **<u>S</u>tyle** option, allows you to search for, or replace, different paragraph styles. This can be useful if you develop a new style and want to change all the text of another style in a document to use your preferred style.

Using the **Special** button, you can search for, and replace, various specified document marks, tabs, hard returns, etc., or a combination of both these and text, as listed in the previous screen dump.

Below we list only two of the many key combinations of special characters that could be typed into the **Fi<u>n</u>d what** and **Replace wi<u>t</u>h** boxes when the **<u>U</u>se wildcards** box is checked.

Type	*To find or replace*
?	Any single character within a pattern. For example, searching for nec?, will find <u>neck</u>, con<u>nect</u>, etc.
*	Any string of characters. For example, searching for c*r, will find such words as <u>cellar</u>, <u>chillier</u>, etc., also parts of words such as <u>character</u>, and combinations of words such as <u>connect, cellar</u>.

Page Breaks

The program automatically inserts a 'soft' page break in a document when a page of typed text is full. To force a manual, or hard page break, either type <Ctrl+Enter> or use the **Insert**, **Break** command and select **Page Break** in the dialogue box, as shown to the left.

Pressing **OK** places a series of dots across the page to indicate the page break (this can only be seen in Normal View, as shown below. If you are in Print View, the second paragraph below appears on the next page. To delete manual page breaks place the cursor on the line of dots, and press the <Del> key. In Print View, place the cursor at the beginning of the second page and press the <BkSp> key.

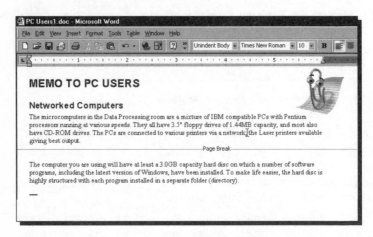

Soft page breaks which are automatically entered by the program at the end of pages, cannot be deleted.

Using the Spell Checker

The package has a very comprehensive spell checker which whenever it thinks it has found a misspelled word, underlines it with a red wavy line. To correct your document, right-click such words for alternatives.

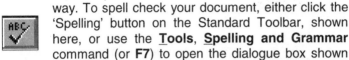

However, the spell checker can also be used in another way. To spell check your document, either click the 'Spelling' button on the Standard Toolbar, shown here, or use the **Tools**, **Spelling and Grammar** command (or **F7**) to open the dialogue box shown below (if necessary, use the **Tools**, **Language**, **Set Language** command, select the correct dictionary and click the **Default** button).

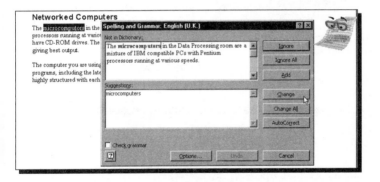

Word starts spell checking from the point of insertion onwards. If you want to spell check the whole document, move the insertion pointer to the beginning of the document before starting. If you want to check a word or paragraph only, highlight it first. Once Word has found a misspelled word, you can either correct it in the Not in Dictionary box, or select a word from the **Suggestions** list.

The main dictionary cannot be edited. However, the system has the ability to add specialised and personal dictionaries with the facility to customise and edit them. If you are using a personal dictionary and choose **Add**, the specified word is added to that dictionary.

Using the Thesaurus

If you are not sure of the meaning of a word, or you want to use an alternative word in your document, then the thesaurus is an indispensable tool. To use the thesaurus, simply place the cursor on the word you want to look up and select **Tools, Language, Thesaurus** command (or press the <Shift+**F7**> key combination). As long as the word is recognised, the following dialogue box will open.

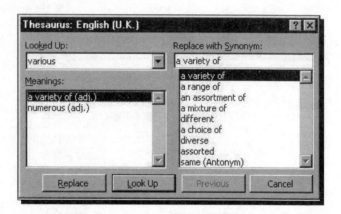

This is very powerful tool. You can see information about an item in the **Meanings** list, or you can look up a synonym in the **Replace with Synonym** list. To change the word in the **Looked Up** text box, select an offered word in either the **Meanings** or the **Replace with Synonym** list box, or type a word directly into the **Replace with Synonym** text box, and press the **Replace** button.

You can use the thesaurus like a simple dictionary by typing any word into the **Replace with Synonym** box and clicking the **Look Up** button. If the word is recognised, lists of its meaning variations and synonyms will be displayed. Pressing the **Replace** button will place the word into the document.

Printing Documents

When Windows was first installed on your computer the printers you intend to use should have been selected, and the SETUP program should have installed the appropriate printer drivers. Before printing for the first time, you would be wise to ensure that your printer is in fact properly installed. To do this, click on **Start** then select **Settings** and click the **Printers** menu option to open the Printers dialogue box shown below.

Here, two printer drivers have been installed; an HP LaserJet 5MP as the 'default' printer and an HP LaserJet 5/5M PostScript. In our case these are both configured to output to a printer via the parallel port LPT1. This refers to the socket at the back of your PC which is connected to your printer. LPT1 is short for Line Printer No. 1. Your selections may, obviously, not be the same.

To see how a printer is configured (whether to print to the parallel port or to a file), select it by clicking its icon, use the **File, Properties** command and click the Details tab of the displayed dialogue box.

Opening a Word Document

Next, return to or reactivate Word and, if the document you

want to print is not in memory, either click the 'Open' button on the Standard Toolbar, or use the **File, Open** command, to display the Open dialogue box shown overleaf.

Use this dialogue box to locate the file (document) you want to print, which will be found on the drive and folder (directory) on which you saved it originally. Select it and click the **Open** button (or double-click its name), to load it into your computer's memory.

To print your document, do one of the following:

- Click the Print icon on the Standard Toolbar, shown here, which prints the document using the current defaults.

- Use the **File, Print** command which opens the 'Print' box, shown below.

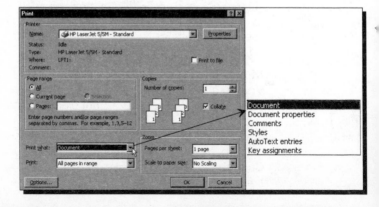

The settings in the Print dialogue box allow you to select the number of copies, and which pages, you want printed. You can also select to print the document, the summary information relating to that document, comments, styles, etc., as shown in the drop-down list also on the previous page.

You can even change the selected printer by clicking the down arrow against the **Printer Name** box which displays the available printers on your system.

Clicking the **Properties** button on the Print dialogue box, displays the Properties dialogue box for the selected printer, shown below, which allows you to select the paper size, orientation needed, paper source, etc.

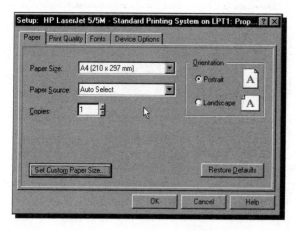

The **Options** button on the Print dialogue box, gives you access to some more advanced print options, such as printing in reverse order, with or without comments, print hidden text or field codes, etc., as shown on the next page.

Clicking the **OK** button on these various multilevel dialogue boxes, causes Word to accept your selections and return you to the previous level dialogue box, until the Print dialogue box is reached. Selecting **OK** on this first level dialogue box, sends print output from Word to your selection, either the printer connected to your computer, or to an encoded file on disc. Selecting **Cancel** or **Close** on any level dialogue box, aborts the selections made at that level.

Do remember that, whenever you change printers, the appearance of your document may change, as Word uses the fonts available with the newly selected printer. This can affect the line lengths, which in turn will affect both the tabulation and pagination of your document.

Before printing to paper, click the Print Preview icon (if not on the Standard Toolbar, click the More Buttons icon or use the **File, Print Preview** command, to see how much of your document will fit on your selected page size. This depends very much on the chosen font. Thus, this option allows you to see the layout of the final printed page, which can save a few trees and equally important to you, a lot of frustration and wear and tear on your printer. To return to your working document from a print preview display, click the **Close** button on its menu bar.

Other enhancements of your document, such as selection of fonts, formatting of text, and pagination, will be discussed in the next chapter.

6

Formatting Word Documents

Formatting involves the appearance of individual words or even characters, the line spacing and alignment of paragraphs, and the overall page layout of the entire document. These functions are carried out in Word in several different ways.

Primary page layout is included in a document's Template and text formatting in a Template's styles. Within any document, however, you can override Paragraph Style formats by applying text formatting and enhancements manually to selected text. To immediately cancel manual formatting, select the text and use the **Edit, Undo** command, or (<Ctrl+Z>). The selected text reverts to its original format. In the long term, you can cancel manual formatting by selecting the text and using the <Shift+Ctrl+N> key stroke. The text then reverts to its style format.

Formatting Text

If you use TrueType fonts, which are automatically installed when you set up Windows, Word uses the same font to display text on the screen and to print on paper. The screen fonts provide a very close approximation of printed characters. TrueType font names are preceded by ℾ in the Font box on the Formatting Bar and in the Font dialogue box which displays when you use the **Format, Font** command.

If you use non-TrueType fonts, then use a screen font that matches your printer font. If a matching font is not available, or if your printer driver does not provide screen font information, Windows chooses the screen font that most closely resembles the printer font.

Originally, the title and subtitle of the **PC Users1** memo, were selected from the default Normal style as 'Heading 1' and 'Heading 3', which were in the 16 and 13 point size Arial typeface, respectively, while the main text was typed in 10 point size Times New Roman.

To change this memo into what appears on the screen dump displayed below, first select the title of the memo and format it to italics, 18 point size Arial and centre it between the margins, then select the subtitle and format it to 14 point size Arial. Both title and subtitle are in bold as part of the definition of their respective paragraph style. Finally select each paragraph of the main body of the memo in turn, and format it to 12 point size Times New Roman. If you can't access these font styles, it will probably be because your printer does not support them, in which case you will need to select other fonts that are supported.

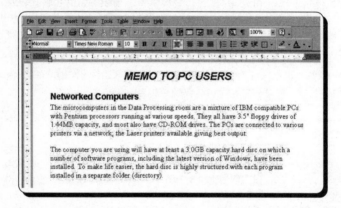

All of this formatting can be achieved by using the buttons on the Formatting Bar (see also the section entitled 'Paragraph Alignment').

As you can see, by moving the Formatting Bar from its former position (to the right of the Standard Toolbar) to just below it (see next section on how to do this), we have exposed more buttons.

Save the result under the new filename **PC Users2**, using the **File, Save As** command.

Moving Toolbars

As we have seen, the default buttons appearing on the two Toolbars below the Menu Bar have distinctive functions. The one to the left is Standard Toolbar, while the one to the right is the Formatting Bar. Each of these two Toolbars is preceded by a vertical handle. Moving the mouse pointer on such a handle, changes it into a small four-headed 'moving' pointer, as shown below.

It is in fact possible to move individual Toolbar sets to any part of the screen, and also change the buttons contained in each. As an example, we will move the Formatting Bar and place it below the Standard Toolbar. To do so, move the mouse pointer on to the vertical handle preceding the set you want to move, and when it changes into the small four-headed pointer press the left mouse button and drag it below its current position. Releasing the mouse button, fixes the bar into its new position, as shown below.

As you can see, additional buttons have appeared on both bars, which previously could not be seen.

To see additional sets of Toolbars, use the **View, Toolbars** command to open up a menu of options, as shown to the left. You can toggle these on and off by clicking on their names. Be careful, however, how many of these you activate, as they take valuable screen space.

Text Enhancements

In Word all manual formatting, including the selection of font, point size, style (bold, italic, highlight, strike-through, hidden and capitals), colour, super/subscript, and various underlines, are carried out by first selecting the text and then executing the formatting command.

The easiest way of activating the formatting commands is from the Formatting Bar. Another way is to use the **Format**, **Font** command, which displays the following dialogue box:

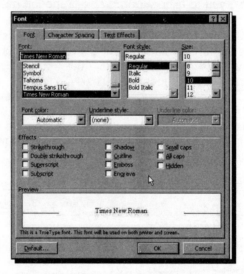

Yet another method is by using quick keys, some of which are listed below:

To Format	*Type*
Bold	Ctrl+B
Italic	Ctrl+I
Underline	Ctrl+U
Word underline	Ctrl+Shift+W
Double underline	Ctrl+Shift+D

There are quick keys to do almost anything, but the problem is remembering them! The ones listed here are the most useful and the easiest to remember.

Paragraph Alignment

Word defines a paragraph, as any text which is followed by a paragraph mark, which is created by pressing the <Enter> key. So single line titles, as well as long typed text, can form paragraphs.

 The paragraph symbol, shown here, is only visible in your text if you have selected it from the Standard Toolbar, or used <Ctrl+*>.

Word allows you to align a paragraph at the left margin (the default), at the right margin, centred between both margins, or justified between both margins. As with most operations there are several ways to perform alignment in Word. Three such methods are:

• Using buttons on the **Formatting Bar**.

• Using keyboard short cuts, when available.

• Using the **Format**, **Paragraph** menu command.

The table below describes the buttons on the Formatting Bar and their keystroke shortcuts.

Buttons on Formatting Bar	Paragraph Alignment	Keystrokes
☰	Left	<Ctrl+L>
☰	Centred	<Ctrl+E>
☰	Right	<Ctrl+R>
☰	Justified	<Ctrl+J>

The display below shows the dialogue box resulting from using the **Fo̲rmat**, **P̲aragraph** command in which you can specify any **L̲eft, R̲ight**, or **Special** indentation required.

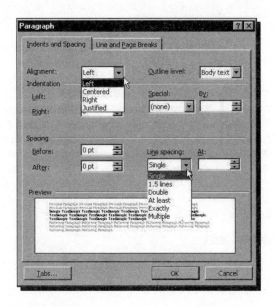

Paragraph Spacing

The above Paragraph dialogue box can also be used to display a paragraph on screen, or print it on paper, in single-line, 1½-line, or double-line spacing. You can even set the spacing to any value you want by using the **At Least** option, as shown on the above screen dump, then specify what interval you want.

The available shortcut keys for paragraph spacing are as follows:

To Format	*Type*
Single-spaced lines	Ctrl+1
One-and-a-half-spaced lines	Ctrl+5
Double-spaced lines	Ctrl+2

Whichever of the above methods is used, formatting can take place either before or after the text is entered. If formatting is selected first, then text will type in the chosen format until a further formatting command is given. If, on the other hand, you choose to enter text and then format it afterwards, you must first select the text to be formatted, then activate the formatting.

Word gives you the choice of 4 units to work with, inches, centimetres, points or picas. These can be selected by using the **Tools**, **Options** command, choosing the **General** tab of the displayed Options dialogue box, and clicking the down arrow against the **Measurement units** list box, shown open here, which is to be found at the bottom of the dialogue box. We selected to work in centimetres from now on.

Indenting Text

Most documents will require some form of paragraph indenting. An indent is the space between the margin and the edge of the text in the paragraph. When an indent is set (on the left or right side of the page), any justification on that side of the page sets at the indent, not the page border.

To illustrate indentation, open the file **PC Users2**, select the first paragraph, and then choose the **Format**, **Paragraph** command. In the **Indentation** field, select 2.5cm for both **Left** and **Right**, as shown on the next page. On clicking **OK**, the first selected paragraph is displayed indented. Our screen dump shows the result of the indentation as well as the settings on the Paragraph dialogue box which caused it.

You can also use the Formatting Bar buttons, shown below, to decrease or increase the indent of a selected text.

 Use this button to decrease indent.

 Use this button to increase indent.

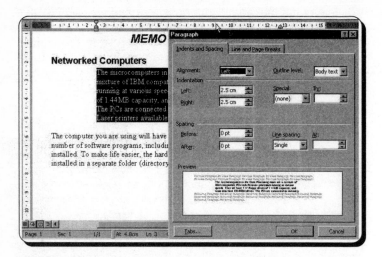

The **Indentation** option in the Paragraph dialogue box, can be used to create 'hanging' indents, where all the lines in a paragraph, including any text on the first line that follows a tab, are indented by a specified amount. This is often used in lists to emphasise certain points.

To illustrate the method, use the **PC Users1** file and add at the end of it the text shown below. After you have typed the text in, save the enlarged memo as **PC Users3**, before going on with formatting the new information.

In Windows you can work with files in three different ways:

Name Description

My Computer Use the My Computer utility which Microsoft have spent much time and effort making as intuitive as possible.

Explorer Use the Windows Explorer, a much-improved version of the older File Manager.

MS-DOS Use an MS-DOS Prompt window if you prefer to and are an expert with the DOS commands.

Saving the work at this stage is done as a precaution in case anything goes wrong with the formatting - it is sometimes much easier to reload a saved file (using the **File, Open** command), than it is to try to unscramble a wrongly formatted document!

Next, highlight the last 4 paragraphs above, use the **Format**, **Paragraph** command, and select 'Hanging' under **Special** and 3 cm under **By**. On clicking the **OK** button, the text formats as shown in the composite screen dump below, but it is still highlighted. To remove the highlighting, click the mouse button anywhere on the page. The second and following lines of the selected paragraphs, should be indented 3 cm from the left margin.

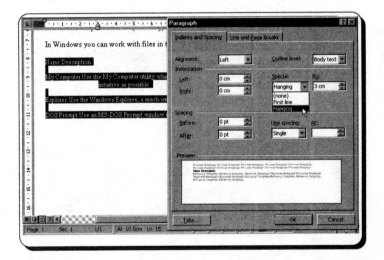

This is still not very inspiring, so to complete the effect we will edit the first lines of each paragraph as follows:

Place the cursor in front of the word 'Description' and press the <Tab> key once. This places the start of the word in the same column as the indented text of the other paragraphs. To complete the effect place tabs before the words 'Use' in the next three paragraphs, until your hanging indents are correct, as shown on the next page.

In Windows you can work with files in three different ways:

Name	Description
My Computer	Use the My Computer utility which Microsoft have spent much time and effort making as intuitive as possible.
Explorer	Use the Windows Explorer, a much-improved version of the older File Manager.
MS-DOS	Use an MS-DOS Prompt window if you prefer to and are an expert with the DOS commands.

This may seem like a complicated rigmarole to go through each time you want the hanging indent effect, but with Word you will eventually set up all your indents, etc., as styles in templates. Then all you do is click in a paragraph to produce them.

 When you finish formatting the document, save it under its current filename either with the **File**, **Save** command (<Ctrl+S>), or by clicking the Save button. This command does not display a dialogue box, so you use it when you do not need to make any changes to the saving operation.

Inserting Bullets

Bullets are small characters you can insert, anywhere you like, in the text of your document to improve visual impact. In Word there are several choices for displaying lists with bullets or numbers. As well as the two Formatting Bar buttons, others are made available through the **Format, Bullets and Numbering** command, which displays the following dialogue box.

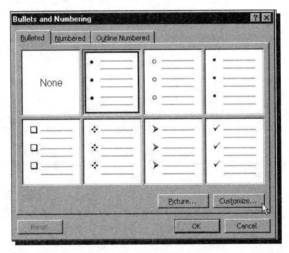

You can select any of the bullets shown here, and then you could click the **Customize** button to change the shape and size of the bullet, or the indentation.

Further, by pressing the **Bullet** button on the Customized Bulleted List dialogue box which would be displayed, you could select any character from the Symbol typeface or other available typefaces.

If you select the **Numbered** or **Outline Numbered** tab, a similar dialogue box is displayed, giving you a choice of several numbering or outline (multilevel) systems.

Once inserted, you can copy, move or cut a bulleted line in the same way as any other text. However, you can not delete a bullet with the <BkSp> or <Del> keys.

Formatting with Page Tabs

You can format text in columns by using tab stops. Word has default left tab stops every 1.27 cm from the left margin, as shown here. This symbol appears on the left edge of the ruler (see below).

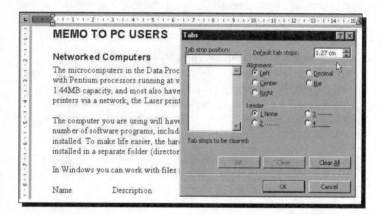

To set tabs, use either the **Format**, **Tabs** command which produces the Tab dialogue box, or click on the tab symbol on the left of the Ruler which cycles through the available tab stops.

The tab stop types available have the following function:

	Button Name	Effect
	Left	Left aligns text after the tab stop.
	Centre	Centres text on tab stop.
	Right	Right aligns text after the tab stop.
	Decimal	Aligns decimal point with tab stop.

To clear the ruler of tab settings press the **Clear All** button in the Tabs dialogue box. When you set a tab stop on the ruler, all default tab stops to the left of the one you are setting are removed. In addition, tab stops apply either to the paragraph containing the cursor, or to any selected paragraphs.

The easiest way to set a tab is to click on the tab type button you want and then point and click at the required position on the lower half of the ruler. To remove an added tab, point to it, click and drag it off the ruler.

If you want tabular text to be separated by characters instead of by spaces, select one of the three available characters from the **Leader** box in the Tabs dialogue box. The options are none (the default), dotted, dashed, or underline. The Contents pages of this book are set with right tabs and dotted leader characters.

Note: As all paragraph formatting, such as tab stops, is placed at the end of a paragraph, if you want to carry the formatting of the current paragraph to the next, press <Enter>. If you don't want formatting to carry on, press the down arrow key instead.

Formatting with Styles

We saw earlier on page 76, how you can format your work using Paragraph Styles, but we confined ourselves to using the default **Normal** style only. In this section we will get to grips with how to create, modify, use, and manage styles.

As mentioned previously, a Paragraph Style is a set of formatting instructions which you save so that you can use it repeatedly within a document or in different documents. A collection of Paragraph Styles can be placed in a Template which could be appropriate for, say, all your memos, so it can be used to preserve uniformity. It maintains consistency and saves time by not having to format each paragraph individually.

Further, should you decide to change a style, all the paragraphs associated with that style reformat automatically. Finally, if you want to provide a pattern for shaping a final document, then you use what is known as a Template. All documents which have not been assigned a document template, use the **Normal.dot** global template, by default.

Paragraph Styles

Paragraph Styles contain paragraph and character formats and a name can be attached to these formatting instructions. From then on, applying the style name is the same as formatting that paragraph with the same instructions.

You can create a style by example, using either the Formatting Bar or the keyboard, or you can create a style from scratch, before you use it, by selecting the **F̲ormat, S̲tyle** menu command. By far the simplest way of creating a style is by example.

Creating Paragraph Styles by Example: Previously, we spent some time manually creating some hanging indents in the last few paragraphs of the **PC Users3** document. To create a style from this previous work, place the insertion pointer in one of these paragraphs, say, in the 'Name Description' line, and highlight the entire name of the existing style in the Formatting Bar's Style box, as shown below.

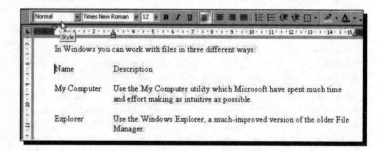

Then, type the new style name you want to create, say, 'Hanging Indent', and press <Enter>.

Finally, highlight the last three paragraphs with hanging indents and change their style to the new 'Hanging Indent', by clicking the mouse in the Style box button and selecting the appropriate style from the displayed list, as shown below. Save the result as **PC Users4**.

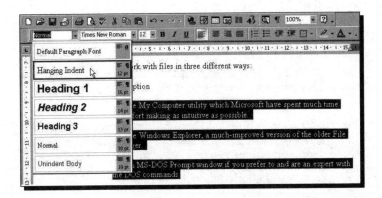

Creating Styles with the Menu Command: You can create, or change, a style before you apply any formatting to a paragraph, by using the **F**o**rmat**, **S**t**yle** command. This displays the Style dialogue box, in which you can choose which style you want to change from the displayed **S**t**yles** list.

Having selected the style you want to change (or not, as the case may be), click the **Modify** button which produces the Modify Style dialogue box. From here you can create a new style, or modify an existing style, by changing the formatting of characters, borders, paragraphs, and tab stops. You can even select which style should follow your current style.

Finally, have a look at Word's built-in styles by selecting **Style** **G**allery from the **F**o**rmat**, **T**h**eme** menu. There are over sixty available styles, one of which might suite your type of document. Try them with the **PC Users4** file open, as it reformats your document on a viewing pane.

Document Templates

A document template provides the overall pattern of your final document. It can contain:

- Styles to control your paragraph and formats.

- Page set-up options.

- Boilerplate text, which is text that remains the same in every document.

- AutoText, which is standard text and graphics that you could insert in a document by typing the name of the AutoText entry.

- Macros, which are programs that can change the menus and key assignments to comply with the type of document you are creating.

- Customised shortcuts, toolbars and menus.

If you don't assign a template to a document, then the default **Normal.dot** template is used by Word. To create a new document template, you either modify an existing one, create one from scratch, or create one based on the formatting of an existing document.

Creating a Document Template

To illustrate the last point above, we will create a simple document template, which we will call **PC User**, based on the formatting of the **PC Users4** document. But first, make sure you have defined the 'Hanging Indent' style as explained earlier.

To create a template based on an existing document do the following:

- Open the existing document.

- Select the **File, Save As** command which displays the Save As dialogue box, shown overleaf.

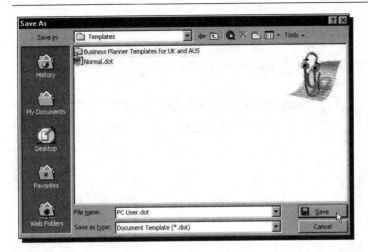

- In the **Save as type** box, select Document Template.

- In the **Save in** box, use the Templates folder which should have opened for you.

- In the **File name** box, type the name of the new template (PC User in our example).

- Press the **Save** button, which opens the template file **PC User.dot** in the Word working area.

- Add the text and graphics you want to appear in all new documents that you base on this template, and *delete* any items (including text) you do not want to appear. In our example, we deleted everything in the document, bar the heading, and added the words 'PC User Group' using **Insert, Picture, WordArt**, to obtain:

- Click the Save icon on the Toolbar, and close the document.

To use the new template, do the following:

- Use the **File**, **New** command which causes the New dialogue box to be displayed, as shown below.

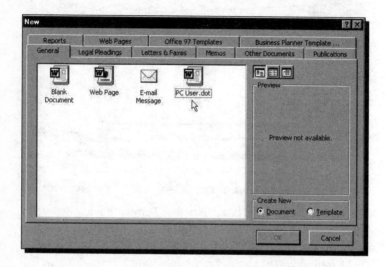

- Click the General tab and select the name of the template you want to use from the displayed list.

- Make sure that the radio button **Document** is selected, and click the **OK** button.

The new document will be using the selected template.

Templates can also contain Macros as well as AutoText; macros allow you to automate Word keystroke actions only, while AutoText speeds up the addition of boilerplate text and graphics into your document. However, the design of these features is beyond the scope of this book.

On the other hand, Word has a series of built-in templates to suit every occasion. These can be found, as seen in the above dialogue box, under the tabs of Letters & Faxes, Memos, Reports, etc. If you upgraded from Office 97, you even have its templates for your use. Try looking at some of these templates.

Special Formatting Features

Word has several special formatting features which force text to override style and style sheet formatting. In what follows, we discuss the most important amongst these.

Changing the Default Character Format

As we have seen, for all new documents Word uses the Times New Roman type font with a 12 points size as the default for the Normal style, which is contained in the Normal template. If the majority of your work demands some different font style or size, then you can change these defaults to suit yourself.

To change the default character formatting, use the **Format**, **Font** command, select the new defaults you want to use, and press the **Default** button, as shown below:

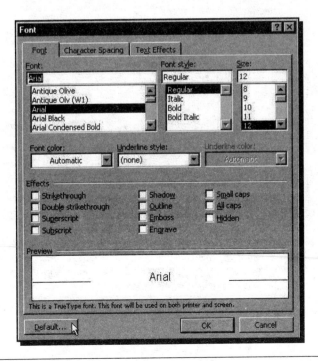

On pressing the **Default** button, The Help Assistant displays the following warning:

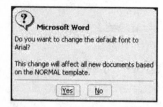

Pressing the **Yes** button, changes the default character settings for this and all subsequent new documents, but does not change already existing ones.

Inserting Special Characters and Symbols

Word has a collection of Symbol fonts, such as the characters produced by the Symbol, Webdings, and Wingdings character sets, from which you can select characters and insert them into your document using the **Insert, Symbol** command. When this command is executed, Word displays the following dialogue box:

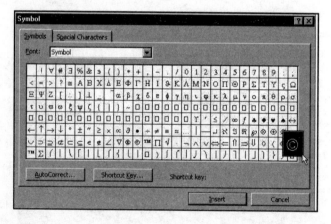

Pressing the down-arrow button next to the **Font** box, reveals the other available character sets. The set showing above is the Symbol set. If you point and click the left mouse button at a character within the set, it selects it and magnifies the selected character. If you double-click the left mouse button, it transfers the selected character to your document at the insertion point.

A Symbol character can be deleted with the <Del> key if you press it twice, or if you press the <BkSp> key once. The advantage of using Symbol is that Word embeds codes in your document which prevent you from changing the character by selecting it and changing to a different font. Thus, this type of formatting overrides any changes you might introduce with a new paragraph formatting.

Inserting Other Special Characters

You can include other special characters in a document, such as optional hyphens, which remain invisible until they are needed to hyphenate a word at the end of a line; non-breaking hyphens, which prevent unwanted hyphenation; non-breaking spaces, which prevent two words from splitting at the end of a line; or opening and closing single quotes.

There are two ways you could use to insert such special characters in your document. One is to click at the **Special Characters** tab of the Symbol dialogue box which reveals a long list of these special characters, as shown below, select one of them and click the **Insert** button. The other way is to use the default key combination (listed against the special characters of the Symbol dialogue box), which does not require you to open it in the first place.

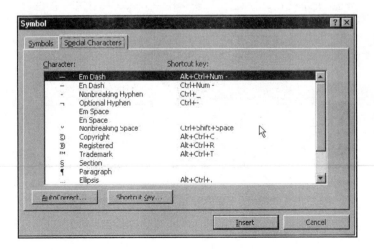

* * *

Word has many more features, far too numerous to mention in the space allocated to this book, although we will be discussing later on how you can use Word to share information with other Microsoft applications and how to use mail merge techniques. What we have tried to do so far, is give you enough basic information so that you can have the confidence to forge ahead and explore the rest of Word's capabilities by yourself.

Perhaps, you might consider exploring page numbering, headers and footers, tables, frames, drawing, and outlining, in that order. We leave it to you. However, if you would prefer to be guided through these topics, then may we suggest you look up the later chapters of the book *Microsoft Word 2000 explained* (BP472), also published by BERNARD BABANI (publishing) Ltd.

* * *

7

The Excel Spreadsheet

Microsoft Excel is a powerful and versatile software package which, over the last few years, has proved its usefulness, not only in the business world, but with scientific and engineering users as well.

The program's power lies in its ability to emulate everything that can be done by the use of pencil, paper and a calculator. Thus, it is an 'electronic spreadsheet' or simply a 'spreadsheet', a name which is also used to describe it and other similar products. Its power is derived from the power of the computer it is running on, and the flexibility and accuracy with which it can deal with the solution of the various applications it is programmed to manage. These can vary from budgeting and forecasting to the solution of complex scientific and engineering problems.

Starting the Excel Program

Excel is started in Windows either by clicking the **Start** button

then selecting **Programs** and clicking on the 'Microsoft Excel' icon on the cascade menu, clicking the Excel icon on the Office Shortcut Bar, or the 'Open Office Document' icon on the Office Shortcut Bar, or by clicking and double-clicking on an Excel workbook file. In the latter case the workbook will be loaded into Excel at the same time.

Whether you have used a previous version of Excel or not, the first time you use the program, it might be a good idea to activate **The Office Assistant** and type *what's new* in the text box, then click **Search**.

This causes the following Help screen to be displayed. Start

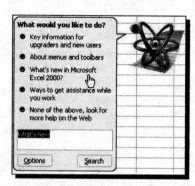

by looking at the 'Key information for upgraders and new users' option, from which you can find out differences between this version of Excel and previous versions of the program. Then, look at the 'What's new in Microsoft Excel 2000' option.

We suggest you spend a little time here browsing through the various help screens. Below, we show the help topics available under 'What's new in Microsoft Excel 2000' so that you can see the wealth of information contained in them.

The Excel Screen

When Excel is loaded, a 'blank' spreadsheet screen displays with a similar Title bar, Menu bar, Toolbar and Formatting bar to those of Word. Obviously there are some differences, but that is to be expected as the two programs serve different purposes.

The opening screen of Excel is shown below. It is perhaps worth looking at the various parts that make up this screen, or window, if only to see how similar it is to that of Word. Excel follows the usual Microsoft Windows conventions with which you should be very familiar by now.

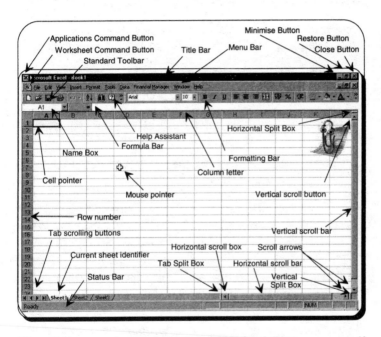

The window as shown above takes up the full screen area. If you click on the application restore button, the top one of the two restore buttons at the top right of the screen, you can make Excel show in a smaller window. This can be useful when you are running several applications at the same time and you want to transfer between them with the mouse.

Note that the Excel window, which in this case displays an empty and untitled book (Book1), has some areas which have identical functions to those of Word (refer to 'The Word Screen' section in Chapter 4), and other areas which have different functions. Below, we describe only the areas that are exclusive to Excel.

Area	*Function*
Name box	Identifies the selected cell (by name or by cell co-ordinates), chart item, or drawing object.
Formula Bar	Can display a number, a label, or the formula behind a result.
Cell pointer	Marks the current cell.
Column letter	The letter that identifies each column.
Row number	The number that identifies each row.
Tab scrolling	Clicking on these buttons, scrolls sheet tabs right or left, when there are more tabs than can be displayed at once.
Current sheet	Shows the current sheet amongst a number of sheets in a file. These are named Sheet1, Sheet2, Sheet3, and so on, by default, but can be changed to, say, North, South, East, and West. Clicking on a sheet tab, moves you to that sheet.
Tab split box	The split box which you drag left to see more of the scroll bar, or right to see more tabs.

Finally, note the location of the horizontal and vertical split boxes. The first is located at the extreme right of the screen above the 'top vertical scroll arrow' button. The second is located at the extreme bottom-right corner of the screen, to the left of the 'right horizontal scroll arrow' button. Both of these split the screen and their use will be discussed later.

Workbook Navigation

When you first enter Excel, the program sets up a series of huge electronic pages, or worksheets, in your computer's memory, many times larger than the small part shown on the screen. Individual cells are identified by column and row location (in that order), with present size extending to 256 columns and 65,536 rows. The columns are labelled from A to Z, followed by AA to AZ, BA to BZ, and so on, to IV, while the rows are numbered from 1 to 65,536.

A worksheet can be thought of as a two-dimensional table made up of rows and columns. The point where a row and column intersect is called a cell, while the reference points of a cell are known as the cell address. The active cell (A1 when you first enter the program) is boxed.

Navigation around the worksheet is achieved by using one of the following keys or key combinations:

- Pressing one of the four arrow keys ($\rightarrow\downarrow\leftarrow\uparrow$) moves the active cell one position right, down, left or up, respectively.

- Pressing the <PgDn> or <PgUp> keys moves the active cell down or up one visible page.

- Pressing the <Ctrl+$\rightarrow$> or <Ctrl+$\downarrow$> key combinations moves the active cell to the extreme right of the worksheet (column IV) or extreme bottom of the worksheet (row 65,536).

- Pressing the <Home> key, moves the active cell to the beginning of a row.

- Pressing the <Ctrl+Home> key combination moves the active cell to the home position, A1.

- Pressing the <Ctrl+End> key combination moves the active cell to the lower right corner of the worksheet's currently used area.

- Pressing the **F5** function key will display the Go To dialogue box shown overleaf.

In the **Go to** box a list of named ranges in the active worksheet (to be discussed shortly) is displayed, or one of the last four references from which you chose the **Go To** command.

In the **Reference** box you type the cell reference or a named range you want to move to.

To move the active cell with a mouse, do the following:

*   Point to the cell you want to move to and click the left mouse button. If the cell is not visible, move the window by clicking on the scroll bar arrowhead that points in the direction you want to move,

*   To move a page at a time, click in the scroll bar itself.

*   For larger moves, drag the box in the scroll bar, but the distances moved will depend on the size of the worksheet.

When you have finished navigating around the worksheet, press the <Ctrl+Home> key combination which will move the active cell to the A1 position (provided you have not fixed titles in any rows or columns or have no hidden rows or columns - more about these later).

Note that the area within which you can move the active cell is referred to as the working area of the worksheet, while the letters and numbers in the border at the top and left of the working area give the 'co-ordinates' of the cells in a worksheet. The location of the active cell is constantly monitored by the 'selection indicator' which is to be found on the extreme left below the lower Toolbar of the application window. As the active cell is moved, this indicator displays its address, as shown on the next page.

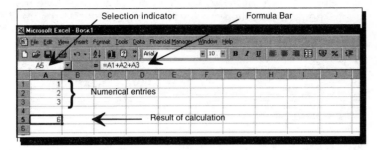

The contents of a cell are displayed above the column letters within what is known as the 'Formula Bar'. If you type text in the active cell, what you type appears in both the Formula Bar and the cell itself.

Typing a formula which is preceded by the equals sign (=) to, say, add the contents of three cells, causes the actual formula to appear in the Formula Bar, while the result of the actual calculation appears in the active cell when the <Enter> key is pressed.

Moving Between Sheets

You can scroll between sheets by clicking one of the arrows situated to the left of Sheet1, as shown below. We have labelled these as 'Tab scrolling buttons'. The inner arrows scroll sheets one at a time in the direction of the arrow, while the outer arrows scroll to the end, or beginning, of the group of available sheets. A sheet is then made current by clicking its tab.

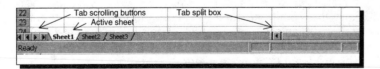

With the keyboard, you can scroll one sheet at a time, and make it active at the same time, by using the <Ctrl+PgDn> key combination. Using <Ctrl+PgUp> scrolls in the reverse direction.

To display more sheet tabs at a time, drag the split box to the right. The reverse action displays less sheet tabs. To rename sheets, double-click at their tab, then type a new name to replace the highlighted name of the particular sheet tab.

To insert a sheet in front of a certain sheet, make that sheet current, then use the **Insert, Worksheet** command sequence. To delete a sheet, make it current and use the **Edit, Delete Sheet** command sequence.

Rearranging Sheet Order

If you need to rearrange the order in which sheets are being held in a workbook, you can do so by dragging a particular sheet to its new position, as shown below.

While you are dragging the tab of the sheet you want to move, the mouse pointer changes to an arrow pointing to a sheet. The small solid arrowhead to the left of the mouse pointer indicates the place where the sheet you are moving will be placed.

Grouping Worksheets

You can select several sheets to group them together so that data entry, editing, or formatting can be made easier and more consistent.

To select adjacent sheets, click the first sheet tab, hold down the <Shift> key and then click the last sheet tab in the group. To select non-adjacent sheets, click the first sheet tab, hold down the <Ctrl> key and then click the other sheet tabs you want to group together.

Selecting sheets in the above manner, causes the word '[Group]' to appear in the Title bar of the active window, and the tabs of the selected sheets to be shown in white. To cancel the selection, click at the tab of any sheet which is not part of the selected group.

Selecting a Range of Cells

To select a range of cells, say, A3:C3, point to cell A3, then

• press the left mouse button, and while holding it pressed, drag the mouse to the right.

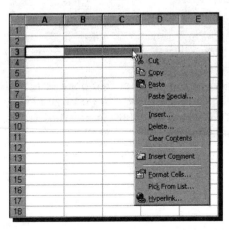

To select a range from the keyboard, first make active the first cell in the range, then

• hold down the <Shift> key and use the right arrow key (→) to highlight the required range.

To select a 3D range, across several sheets, select the range in the first sheet, then

• release the mouse button, hold down the <Shift> key, and click the Tab of the last sheet in the range.

Shortcut Menus

While a range of cells in a sheet is selected, or a group of sheets is active, you can access a shortcut menu of relevant commands by pressing the right mouse button. This produces a shortcut menu, as shown here, of the most common commands relevant to what you are doing at the time.

Viewing Multiple Workbook Sheets

To see more clearly what you are doing when working with multiple workbook sheets, type the text '1st' in location A1 of Sheet1, the text '2nd' in Sheet2, and so on (to add extra sheets in a workbook, use the **Insert, Worksheet** command). Then use the **Window, New Window** command to add three extra windows to your worksheet. Next, use the **Window, Arrange, Tiled** command to display the four sheets as shown below. What we have done below is to make active Sheet1 in Book1:1, Sheet2 in Book1:2, and so on, to demonstrate that each window contains all four sheets.

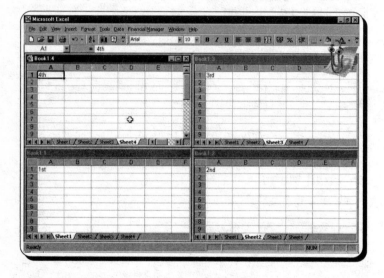

To move from one window to another, simply point with the mouse to the cell of the window you want to go to and click the left mouse button. To display a different sheet in each window, go to a window and click the sheet's tab.

To return to single-window view mode from a tiled or cascade mode, click the maximise button of the active window.

Entering Information

We will now investigate how information can be entered into a worksheet. But first, make sure you are in Sheet1, then return to the Home (A1) position, by pressing the <Ctrl+Home> key combination, then type the words:

```
Project Analysis
```

As you type, the characters appear in both the 'Formula Bar' and the active cell. If you make a mistake, press the <BkSp> key to erase the previous letter or the <Esc> key to start again. When you have finished, press <Enter>.

Note that what you have just typed in has been entered in cell A1, even though the whole of the word ANALYSIS appears to be in cell B1. If you use the right arrow key to move the active cell to B1 you will see that the cell is indeed empty.

Typing any letter at the beginning of an entry into a cell results in a 'text' entry being formed automatically, otherwise known as a 'label'. If the length of the text is longer than the width of a cell, it will continue into the next cell to the right of the current active cell, provided that cell is empty, otherwise the displayed information will be truncated.

To edit information already in a cell, either

- double-click the cell in question, or

- make that cell the active cell and press the **F2** function key.

The cursor keys, the <Home> and <End> keys, as well as the <Ins> and <Del> keys can be used to move the cursor and/or edit information as required.

You can also 'undo' the last 16 actions carried out since the program was last in the **Ready** mode, by either using the **Edit, Undo Entry** command (<Ctrl+Z>), or clicking the Undo button.

Next, move the active cell to B3 and type

```
Jan
```

Pressing the right arrow key (→) will automatically enter the typed information into the cell and also move the active cell one cell to the right, in this case to C3. Now type

```
Feb
```

and press <Enter>.

The looks of a worksheet can be enhanced somewhat by using different types of borders around specific cells. To do this, first select the range of cells, then click at the down arrow of the Borders icon on the Formatting Toolbar, shown here, which displays twelve different types of borders, as shown below.

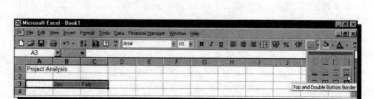

In our example, we have selected the cell range A3:C3, then we chose the 8th border from the display table.

Next, move to cell A4 and type the label Income, then enter the numbers 14000 and 15000 in cells B4 and C4, respectively, as shown below, but note that by default the labels 'Jan' and 'Feb' are left justified, while the numbers are right justified.

	A	B	C	D	E	F	G	H
1	PROJECT ANALYSIS							
2								
3		Jan	Feb					
4	Income	14000	15000		⊕			
5								

Changing Text Alignment and Fonts

One way of improving the looks of this worksheet is to also right justify the text 'Jan' and 'Feb' within their respective cells. To do this, move the active cell to B3 and select the range B3 to C3 by dragging the mouse, then either click the 'Align Right' icon, shown here, or choose the **Format**, **Cells** command, then select the **Alignment** tab from the displayed Format Cells dialogue box, shown below, click the down-arrow against the **Horizontal** text box, highlight **Right** from the drop-down menu options, and press **OK**.

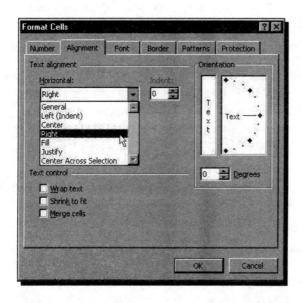

No matter which method you choose, the text should now appear right justified within their cells. However, although the latter method is lengthier, it nevertheless provides you with greater flexibility in displaying text, both in terms of position and orientation.

We could further improve the looks of our worksheet by choosing a different font for the heading 'Project Analysis'. To achieve this, select cell A1, then click on the down arrow against the Font Size button on the Formatting Bar, to reveal the band of available point sizes for the selected font, as shown overleaf. From this band, choose 14, then click in succession the 'Bold' and 'Italic' icons.

Finally, since the numbers in cells B4 to C4 represent money, it would be better if these were prefixed with the £ sign. To do this, select the cell range B4:C4, then either click the 'Currency' button on the Formatting Bar, shown here, or choose the **Format, Style** command and select **Currency** from the list under **Style name** in the displayed Style dialogue box.

The numbers within the chosen range will now be displayed in currency form, and the width of the cells will automatically adjust to accommodate them, if they are too long which is the case in our example.

To see the actual new width of, say column C4, place the mouse pointer, as shown, to the right of the column letter on the dividing line. When the mouse pointer changes to the

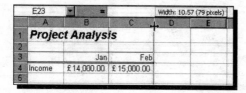

shape shown here, press the left mouse button. The current width will then display within a pop-up text box as 79 pixels, increased from the default column width of 64 pixels.

This new width accommodates our numbers exactly, but we might like to increase it to, say, 82 pixels so that it looks better. To do this, place the mouse pointer in between the column letters, and drag the pointer to the right, until the width of the column displays as 82 pixels, which also happens to be 11 characters wide.

Saving a Workbook

Now, let us assume that we would like to stop at this point, but would also like to save the work entered so far before leaving the program. First, return to the Home position by pressing <Ctrl+Home>. This is good practice because the position of the cell pointer at the time of saving the file is preserved. For example, had you placed the cell pointer well beyond the data entry area of your worksheet at the time of saving, when you later opened this worksheet you might be confused to see empty cells surrounding the cell pointer - you might think that you have opened an empty worksheet.

Next, choose the **File, Save** command to reveal the Save As dialogue box. You could select to save your work in the default **My Documents** folder, or create a suitably named folder using the Create New Folder button on the Save As dialogue box, shown below.

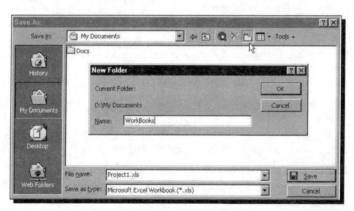

We used this facility to create a folder called **WorkBooks** within the **My Documents** folder.

To save our work currently in memory, we selected the **WorkBooks** folder in the **Save in** field of the Save As dialogue box, then moved the cursor into the **File name** box, and typed **Project 1**. We suggest you do the same.

The file will be saved in the default file type *Microsoft Excel Workbook*, as displayed in the **Save as type** box. Excel adds the file extension **.xls** automatically and uses it to identify it.

By clicking the **Save as type** button at the bottom of the Save As dialogue box, you can save your work in a variety of other formats, including Web Page (HTML), Template, and earlier versions of Excel.

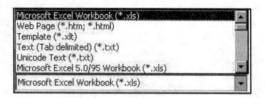

If you want to create backup files or provide password protection to your file, click the down-arrow against the **Tools** button at the top of the Save As dialogue box, and select **General Options** from the displayed drop down menu. This opens the Save Options dialogue box, shown in the middle of the composite screen dump below. Fill in this dialogue box appropriately and press the **OK** button.

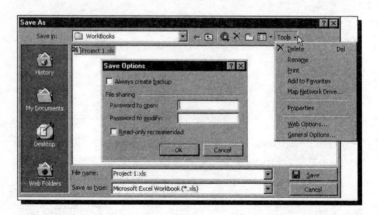

Finally, pressing the **Save** button causes your work to be saved under the chosen filename.

Opening a Workbook

 An already saved workbook, or file, can be opened by either clicking at the 'Open' icon, shown here, or selecting the **File, Open** command which displays the Open dialogue box. Excel asks for a filename to open, with the default *Microsoft Excel Files* being displayed in the **Files of type** box, as shown below. If the file was saved, select it by clicking its name in the list box, then click the **Open** button.

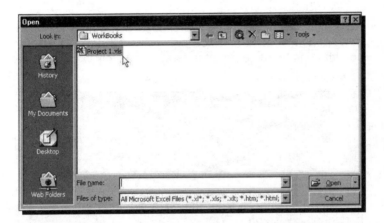

If you haven't saved it, don't worry as you could just as easily start afresh.

If you want to change the logged drive, click the down-arrow against the **Look in** box, of the Open dialogue box, and select the appropriate drive from the drop-down list, as shown here for our computer. In your case, this list will most certainly be different.

Exiting Excel

To exit Excel, close any displayed dialogue boxes by clicking the **Cancel** button, and make sure that the word **Ready** is displayed on the status bar (press the <Esc> key until it does), and either

- choose the **File, Exit** command,
- use the <Alt+F4> key combination, or
- click the Close button.

No matter which command you choose, if you have changed any opened worksheet, Excel will warn you and will ask for confirmation before exiting the program, as follows.

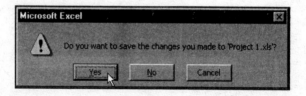

If you do not want to save the changes, then press the **No** button, otherwise press **Yes**.

8

Filling in a Worksheet

We will use, as an example of how a worksheet can be built up, the few entries on 'Project Analysis' from the previous chapter. If you have saved **Project 1**, then either click the Open button, or use the **File, Open** command, then highlight its filename in the Open dialogue box, and click the **OK** button. If you haven't saved it, don't worry as you could just as easily start afresh.

Next, either double-click on the contents of a cell to edit existing entries, or simply retype the contents of cells, so that your worksheet looks as near as possible to the one below. For formatting details, see below and the next page.

	A	B	C	D	E	F	G	H	I
1	*Project Analysis: Adept Consultants Ltd.*								
2									
3		Jan	Feb	Mar	1st Quarter				
4	Income	£ 14,000.00	£ 15,000.00	£ 16,000.00	£ 45,000.00				
5	Costs:								
6	Wages	2000	3000	4000					
7	Travel	400	500	600					
8	Rent	300	300	300					
9	Heat/Light	150	200	130					
10	Phone/Fax	250	300	350					
11	Adverts	1100	1200	1300					
12	Total Costs								
13	Profit								
14	Cumulative								
15									

The lines, like the double line stretching from A3 to E3 were entered by first selecting the cell range A3:E3, then clicking the down-arrow of the 'Borders' icon on the Formatting Bar, and selecting the appropriate border from the 12 displayed options.

Formatting Entries

The information in cell A1 (Project Analysis: Adept Consultants Ltd.) was entered left justified and formatted by clicking on the 'Font Size' button on the Formatting Bar, and

  selecting 14 point font size from the band of available font sizes, then clicking in succession the 'Bold' and 'Italic' icons, shown to the left.

The text in the cell block B3:E3 was formatted by first

 selecting the range and then clicking the 'Centre' alignment icon on the Formatting Bar, so the text within the range was displayed centre justified.

The numbers within the cell block B4:E4 were formatted by first selecting the range, then clicking the 'Currency' icon on

the Formatting Bar, shown here, so the numbers appeared with two digits after the decimal point and prefixed with the £ sign.

All the text appearing in column A (apart from that in cell A1) was just typed in (left justified), as shown in the screen dump on the previous page. The width of all the columns A to E was adjusted to 11 characters; a quick way of doing this is to select one row of these columns, then use the **Format, Column, Width** command, and type 11 in the displayed box.

Filling a Range by Example

To fill a range by example, select the first cell of a range,

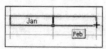 point at the bottom right corner of the cell and when the mouse pointer changes to a small cross, drag the mouse in the required direction to fill the range.

In the above case, we started with a cell containing the abbreviation 'Jan'. The next cell to the right will automatically fill with the text 'Feb' (Excel anticipates that you want to fill cells by example with the abbreviations for months, and does it for you). Not only that, but it also copies the format of the selected range forward.

Entering Text, Numbers and Formulae

Excel allows you to format both text (labels) and numbers in any way you choose. For example, you can have numbers centre justified in their cells.

When text, a number, a formula, or an Excel function is entered into a cell, or reference is made to the contents of a cell by the cell address, then the content of the status bar changes from **Ready** to **Enter**. This status can be changed back to **Ready** by either completing an entry and pressing <Enter> or one of the arrow keys, or by pressing <Esc>.

We can find the 1st quarter total income from consultancy, by activating cell E4, typing

    =b4+c4+d4

and pressing <Enter>. The total first quarter income is added, using the above formula, and the result is placed in cell E4.

Now complete the insertion into the spreadsheet of the various amounts under 'costs' and then choose the **File, Save As** command to save the resultant worksheet under the filename **Project 2**, before going on any further. Remember that saving your work on disc often enough is a good thing to get used to, as even the shortest power cut can cause the loss of hours of hard work!

Using Functions

In our example, writing a formula that adds the contents of three columns is not too difficult or lengthy a task. But imagine having to add 20 columns! For this reason Excel has an inbuilt summation function which can be used to add any number of columns (or rows). But before we continue, it is time to move the Formatting Bar to a position below the Standard Toolbar (see page 107 on how to do this).

To illustrate how this and other functions can be used, activate cell E4 and first press <Del> to clear the cell of its formula, then click the Paste Function button, shown here, on the Standard Toolbar. If the function you require appears on the displayed dialogue box under **Function name**, choose it, otherwise select the appropriate class from the list under **Function category**.

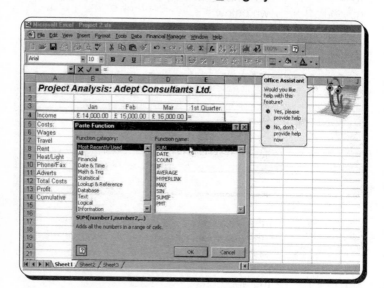

Choosing the **SUM** function, inserts the entry SUM(B4:D4) in the Edit line, as shown below. Clicking the **OK** button, causes this function to be pasted into cell E4, adding all the numbers in the range.

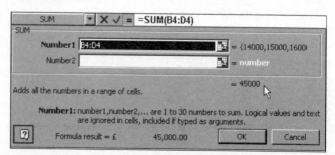

Using the AutoSum Icon

With addition, there is a better and quicker way of letting Excel work out the desired result. To illustrate this, select the cell range B6:E12, which contains the 'Costs' we would like to add up. To add these in both the horizontal and vertical direction, we include in the selected range an empty column to the right of the numbers and an empty row below the numbers, as shown below.

	A	B	C	D	E	F	G	H
1	Project Analysis: Adept Consultants Ltd.							
2								
3		Jan	Feb	Mar	1st Quarter			
4	Income	£ 14,000.00	£ 15,000.00	£ 16,000.00	£ 45,000.00			
5	Costs:							
6	Wages	2000	3000	4000				
7	Travel	400	500	600				
8	Rent	300	300	300				
9	Heat/Light	150	200	130				
10	Phone/Fax	250	300	350				
11	Adverts	1100	1200	1300				
12	Total Costs							
13	Profit							
14	Cumulative							

Pressing the 'AutoSum' icon, shown here, inserts the result of the summations in the empty column and row, as shown below. The selected range remains selected so that any other formatting can be applied by simply pressing the appropriate icon button.

	A	B	C	D	E	F	G	H
1	Project Analysis: Adept Consultants Ltd.							
2								
3		Jan	Feb	Mar	1st Quarter			
4	Income	£ 14,000.00	£ 15,000.00	£ 16,000.00	£ 45,000.00			
5	Costs:							
6	Wages	2000	3000	4000	9000			
7	Travel	400	500	600	1500			
8	Rent	300	300	300	900			
9	Heat/Light	150	200	130	480			
10	Phone/Fax	250	300	350	900			
11	Adverts	1100	1200	1300	3600			
12	Total Costs	4200	5500	6680	16380			

Now complete the insertion of formulae in the rest of the worksheet, noting that 'Profit', in B13, is the difference between 'Income' and 'Total Cost', calculated by the formula **=b4-b12**. To complete the entry, this formula should be copied using the 'fill by example' method into the three cells to its right.

The 'Cumulative' entry in cell B14 should be a simple reference to cell B13, that is **=b13**, while in cell C14 it should be **=b14+b13**. Similarly, the latter formula is copied into cell D14 using the 'fill by example' method.

Next, format the entire range B6:E12 by selecting the range and clicking the 'Currency' button.

If you make any mistakes and copy formats or information into cells you did not mean to, use the **Edit, Undo** command or click the Undo button which allows you to selectively undo what you were just doing. To blank the contents within a range of cells, first select the range, then press the <Del> key.

The worksheet, up to this point, should look as follows:

	A	B	C	D	E	F	G	H
1	*Project Analysis: Adept Consultants Ltd.*							
2								
3		Jan	Feb	Mar	1st Quarter			
4	Income	£ 14,000.00	£ 15,000.00	£ 16,000.00	£ 45,000.00			
5	Costs:							
6	Wages	£ 2,000.00	£ 3,000.00	£ 4,000.00	£ 9,000.00			
7	Travel	£ 400.00	£ 500.00	£ 600.00	£ 1,500.00			
8	Rent	£ 300.00	£ 300.00	£ 300.00	£ 900.00			
9	Heat/Light	£ 150.00	£ 200.00	£ 130.00	£ 480.00			
10	Phone/Fax	£ 250.00	£ 300.00	£ 350.00	£ 900.00			
11	Adverts	£ 1,100.00	£ 1,200.00	£ 1,300.00	£ 3,600.00			
12	Total Costs	£ 4,200.00	£ 5,500.00	£ 6,680.00	£ 16,380.00			
13	Profit	£ 9,800.00	£ 9,500.00	£ 9,320.00	£ 28,620.00			
14	Cumulative	£ 9,800.00	£ 19,300.00	£ 28,620.00				
15								

Finally, use the **File, Save As** command to save your work under the filename **Project 3**.

Printing a Worksheet

To print a worksheet, make sure that the printer you propose to use was defined when you first installed Windows.

If you have named more than one printer in your original installation of Windows, and want to select a printer other than your original first choice, then select the **File, Print** (or <Ctrl+P> command, click the down-arrow against the **Name** box on the displayed Print dialogue box and select the required printer, as shown below.

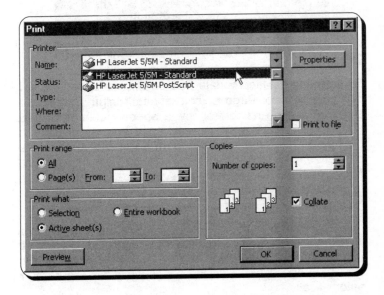

If you want to change the paper size, print orientation or printer resolution, click the **Properties** button on the Print dialogue box. These and other changes to the appearance of the printout can also be made by choosing the **File, Page Setup** command which causes the Page Setup dialogue box to be displayed, as shown overleaf.

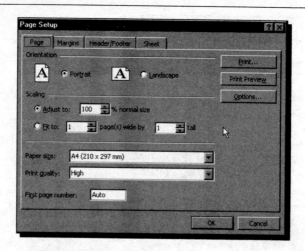

By selecting the appropriate Tab on this dialogue box, you can change your **Page** settings, page **Margins**, specify a **Header/Footer**, and control how a **Sheet** should be printed. Each Tab displays a different dialogue box, appropriate to the function at hand. In the **Header/Footer** dialogue box you can even click the down-arrow against the Header and Footer boxes to display a suggested list for these, appropriate to the work you are doing, the person responsible for it and even the date it is being carried out! Try it.

A very useful feature of Excel is the **Scaling** facility shown in the above dialogue box. You can print actual size or a percentage of it, or you can choose to fit your worksheet on to one page which allows Excel to scale your work automatically.

To preview a worksheet, click the 'Print Preview' icon on the Standard Toolbar, shown here, or click the **Print Preview** button on the Page Setup dialogue box, or the **Preview** button on the Print dialogue box. You can even use the **File, Print Preview** command!

The idea of all these preview choices is to make it easy for you to see your work on screen before committing it to paper, thus saving a few more trees!

Enhancing a Worksheet

You can make your work look more professional by adopting
various enhancements, such as single and double line cell
borders, shading certain cells, and adding meaningful
headers and footers.

However, with Excel you can easily select a predefined
style to display your work on both the screen and on paper.
To do this, place the active cell within the table (or range) you
want to format, say C5, then select the **Format, AutoFormat**
which will cause the following dialogue box to appear on the
screen, displaying a sample of the chosen table format. In
this way you can choose what best suits your needs. We
selected 'Classic 2' and pressed **OK**.

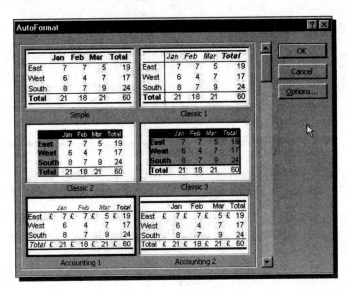

Next, reduce the title of the worksheet to 'Project Analysis',
then centre it within the range A1:E1, by first
selecting the range, then clicking the 'Merge and
Centre' icon, shown here, which causes the title to
centre within the specified range.

Finally, save the worksheet as **Project 4**, before going on.

Header and Footer Icons and Codes

With the help of header and footer icons and their codes, shown below, you can position text or automatically insert information at the top or bottom of a report printout.

To add a header to our printed example, use the **File, Page Setup** command and click first the **Header/Footer** Tab, then the **Custom Header** button and type the information displayed below in the **Left section** and **Right section** of the Header box.

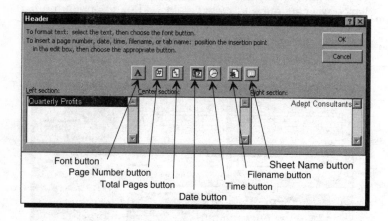

While the insertion pointer is in, say, the **Centre section** of the Header box, pointing and clicking on the 'Sheet Name' button, inserts the &[Tab] code which has the effect of inserting the sheet name of the current active sheet at the time of printing. The first icon button displays the Font dialogue box, while the others display the following codes:

Code	*Action*
&[Page]	Inserts a page number.
&[Pages]	Inserts the total number of pages.
&[Date]	Inserts the current date.
&[Time]	Inserts the current time.
&[File]	Inserts the filename of the current workbook.

Setting a Print Area

To choose a smaller print area than the current worksheet, select the required area by highlighting the starting cell of the area and dragging the mouse, or using the **<Shift+Arrows>**, to highlight the block, and use the **File, Print** command which displays the following dialogue box:

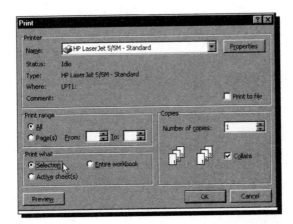

Choose the **Selection** button in the **Print What** box, and either click the **Preview** or the **OK** button to preview your report on screen or print it on paper. Once in preview mode, the following icons are available to you.

The first two allow you to change sheets, while the next one allows you to review your print output magnified or at full page size - when in full page size, the mouse pointer looks like a magnifying glass, as above. The next four icons can be used to print, change page settings, display and change the margins, or adjust the page size by dragging the page breaks to a new position. To return to normal view, click the **Close** button.

Another way to set the area to print is using the **File, Print Area, Set Print Area** menu command. To print selected sheets or the entire workbook, click the appropriate button in the **Print What** box of the Print dialogue box.

The default selection in the **Print What** box is **Active sheet(s)** which is also what will be printed out if you click the 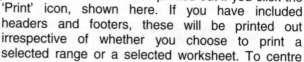 'Print' icon, shown here. If you have included headers and footers, these will be printed out irrespective of whether you choose to print a selected range or a selected worksheet. To centre the page horizontally on the paper, use the **File, Page Setup** command, click the Margins tab and select the option. Finally, printing our worksheet, produces the following page:

Quarterly Profits   Sheet1   Adept Consultants

Project Analysis

	Jan	Feb	Mar	1st Quarter
Income	£14,000.00	£15,000.00	£16,000.00	£45,000.00
Costs:				
Wages	£ 2,000.00	£ 3,000.00	£ 4,000.00	£ 9,000.00
Travel	£ 400.00	£ 500.00	£ 600.00	£ 1,500.00
Rent	£ 300.00	£ 300.00	£ 300.00	£ 900.00
Heat/Light	£ 150.00	£ 200.00	£ 130.00	£ 480.00
Phone/Fax	£ 250.00	£ 300.00	£ 350.00	£ 900.00
Adverts	£ 1,100.00	£ 1,200.00	£ 1,300.00	£ 3,600.00
Total Costs	£ 4,200.00	£ 5,500.00	£ 6,680.00	£16,380.00
Profit	£ 9,800.00	£ 9,500.00	£ 9,320.00	£28,620.00
Cumulative	£ 9,800.00	£19,300.00	£28,620.00	

3-Dimensional Worksheets

In Excel, a Workbook is a 3-dimensional file made up with a series of flat 2-dimensional sheets stacked 'on top of each other'. Each sheet is the same size, and in itself, behaves the same as the more ordinary worksheets. As mentioned previously, each separate sheet in a file has its own Tab identifier at the bottom of the screen. Ranges can be set to span several different sheets to build up 3-dimensional blocks of data. These blocks can then be manipulated, copied, or moved to other locations in the file. A cell can reference any other cell in the file, no matter what sheet it is on, and an extended range of functions can be used to process these 3-dimensional ranges.

Manipulating Ranges

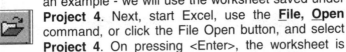

The best way to demonstrate a new idea is to work through an example - we will use the worksheet saved under **Project 4**. Next, start Excel, use the **File, Open** command, or click the File Open button, and select **Project 4**. On pressing <Enter>, the worksheet is displayed on the screen as shown on the facing page.

Copying Sheets in a Workbook

We will now fill another three sheets behind the present one, in order to include information about ADEPT Consultants' trading during the other three quarters of the year. The easiest way of doing this is by copying the information in Sheet1, including the formatting and the entered formulae, onto the other three sheets, then edit the numerical information in these appropriately.

To simplify this operation, Excel has a facility which allows you to copy a sheet into a workbook. There are two ways of doing this: (a) with the mouse, or (b) using the menus.

With the mouse, make the sheet you want to copy the current sheet, then press the <Ctrl> key, and while keeping it pressed, point with the mouse on the Tab of Sheet1 and drag it to the right, as shown overleaf.

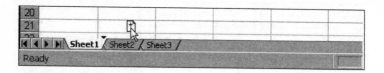

A small black triangle indicates the place where the copy will be inserted, as shown above. If you insert a copy, say before Sheet2, when you release the mouse button the inserted sheet will be given the name Sheet1(2), while inserting a second copy before Sheet2 will be given the name Sheet1(3).

To copy a sheet with the menus, select the **Edit, Move or Copy Sheet** command, then highlight Sheet2 in the **Before**

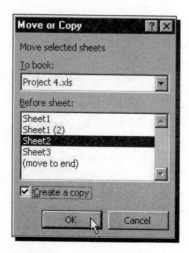

sheet list of the displayed dialogue box, then check the **Create a copy** option at the bottom of the dialogue box, and press the **OK** button. Sheet1(2) will be inserted in the Workbook, in the above case.

When you have three copies placed, double-click the Tabs of Sheet1 and the three new sheets and change their names to 'Quarter 1', 'Quarter 2', 'Quarter 3' and 'Quarter 4', respectively, as shown below.

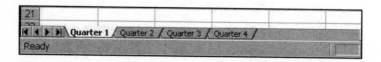

The contents of the second sheet should be as shown on the next page.

	A	B	C	D	E	F
1	**Project Analysis 2nd Quarter**					
2						
3		Apr	May	Jun	2nd Quarter	
4	Income	£ 15,500.00	£ 16,000.00	£ 16,500.00	£ 48,000.00	
5	Costs:					
6	Wages	£ 3,500.00	£ 4,000.00	£ 4,500.00	£ 12,000.00	
7	Travel	£ 500.00	£ 550.00	£ 580.00	£ 1,630.00	
8	Rent	£ 300.00	£ 300.00	£ 300.00	£ 900.00	
9	Heat/Light	£ 150.00	£ 120.00	£ 100.00	£ 370.00	
10	Phone/Fax	£ 300.00	£ 350.00	£ 400.00	£ 1,050.00	
11	Adverts	£ 1,250.00	£ 1,300.00	£ 1,350.00	£ 3,900.00	
12	Total Costs	£ 6,000.00	£ 6,620.00	£ 7,230.00	£ 19,850.00	
13	Profit	£ 9,500.00	£ 9,380.00	£ 9,270.00	£ 28,150.00	
14	Cumulative	£ 9,500.00	£ 18,880.00	£ 28,150.00		
15						
16						
17						
18						
19						

Quarter 1 \ Quarter 2 / Quarter 3 / Quarter 4 /

The easiest way to enter these 2nd Quarter results is to edit the copied data (from Quarter 1) by either using the EDIT key (**F2**), or double-clicking the cell you want to edit. You should now be in a position to complete editing this sheet. Be extra careful, from now on, to check the identification Tab at the bottom of the screen, so as not to get the sheets mixed up. You do not want to spend time editing the wrong worksheet!

After building up the four worksheets (one for each quarter - see below for details on the 3rd and 4th quarters) save the file as **Project 5**.

	Jul	Aug	Sep	Oct	Nov	Dec
Income	17,000	17,500	18,000	18,500	19,000	19,500
Costs:						
Wages	4,000	4,500	5,000	4,500	5,000	5,500
Travel	600	650	680	630	670	700
Rent	300	300	300	300	300	300
Heat/Light	50	80	120	160	200	250
Phone/Fax	350	380	420	400	420	450
Adverts	1,400	1,450	1,500	1,480	1,500	1,530

Linking Sheets

A consolidation sheet could be placed in front of our 'stack' of data sheets to show a full year's results, by making a copy of the 1st Quarter sheet and placing it in front of it. Next, delete the entries in columns B to E, and name it 'Consolidation'.

We are now in a position to link the consolidation sheet to the other quarterly data sheets so that the information contained on them is automatically summarised and updated on it. The quarter totals in columns E of sheets Quarter 1, Quarter 2, Quarter 3, and Quarter 4, can be copied in turn to the clipboard using the **Edit, Copy** command, and then pasted to the appropriate column of the Consolidation sheet with the use of the **Edit, Paste Special** command and clicking the **Paste Link** button on the displayed dialogue box.

Note: Empty cells linked with this method, like those in cells E5 of each quarter, appear as 0 (zero) in the Consolidation sheet, and cannot be removed. To correct this, either copy each column E of each quarter in two stages; E3:E4, then E6:E13, or check the **Skip blanks** box in the Paste Special dialogue box. If you choose the latter method, you will have to increase the width of the relevant columns manually.

Next, insert appropriate formulae in row 14 to correctly calculate the cumulative values in the Consolidation sheet. The result should be as follows:

	A	B	C	D	E	F	G	H
1	*Project Analysis - Year Summary*							
2								
3		1st Quarter	2nd Quarter	3rd Quarter	4th Quarter			
4	Income	£ 45,000.00	£ 48,000.00	£ 52,500.00	£ 57,000.00			
5	Costs:							
6	Wages	£ 9,000.00	£ 12,000.00	£ 13,500.00	£ 15,000.00			
7	Travel	£ 1,500.00	£ 1,630.00	£ 1,930.00	£ 2,000.00			
8	Rent	£ 900.00	£ 900.00	£ 900.00	£ 900.00			
9	Heat/Light	£ 480.00	£ 370.00	£ 250.00	£ 610.00			
10	Phone/Fax	£ 900.00	£ 1,050.00	£ 1,150.00	£ 1,270.00			
11	Adverts	£ 3,600.00	£ 3,900.00	£ 4,350.00	£ 4,510.00			
12	Total Costs	£ 16,380.00	£ 19,850.00	£ 22,080.00	£ 24,290.00			
13	*Profit*	£ 28,620.00	£ 28,150.00	£ 30,420.00	£ 32,710.00			
14	*Cumulative*	£ 28,620.00	£ 56,770.00	£ 87,190.00	£ 119,900.00			
15								

Finally, save the resultant workbook as **Project 6**.

Relative and Absolute Cell Addresses

Entering a mathematical expression into Excel, such as the formula in cell C14 which was

=B14+C13

causes Excel to interpret it as 'add the contents of cell one column to the left of the current position, to the contents of cell one row above the current position'. In this way, when the formula was later copied into cell address D14, the contents of the cell relative to the left position of D14 (i.e. C14) and the contents of the cell one row above it (i.e. D13) were used, instead of the original cell addresses entered in C14. This is relative addressing.

To see the effect of relative versus absolute addressing, copy the formula in cell C14 into C17, as shown below:

C17	▼	=	=B17+C16		
	A	B	C	D	E	F

	A	B	C	D	E
1	*Project Analysis - Year Summary*				
2					
3		**1st Quarter**	**2nd Quarter**	**3rd Quarter**	**4th Quarter**
4	Income	£ 45,000.00	£ 48,000.00	£ 52,500.00	£ 57,000.00
5	Costs:				
6	Wages	£ 9,000.00	£ 12,000.00	£ 13,500.00	£ 15,000.00
7	Travel	£ 1,500.00	£ 1,630.00	£ 1,930.00	£ 2,000.00
8	Rent	£ 900.00	£ 900.00	£ 900.00	£ 900.00
9	Heat/Light	£ 480.00	£ 370.00	£ 250.00	£ 610.00
10	Phone/Fax	£ 900.00	£ 1,050.00	£ 1,150.00	£ 1,270.00
11	Adverts	£ 3,600.00	£ 3,900.00	£ 4,350.00	£ 4,510.00
12	Total Costs	£ 16,380.00	£ 19,850.00	£ 22,080.00	£ 24,290.00
13	*Profit*	£ 28,620.00	£ 28,150.00	£ 30,420.00	£ 32,710.00
14	*Cumulative*	£ 28,620.00	£ 56,770.00	£ 87,190.00	£ 119,900.00
15					
16					
17			£ -	✥	

Note that in cell C14 the formula was =B14+C13. However, when copied into cell C17 the formula appears as

=B17+C16

This is because it has been interpreted as relative addressing. In this case, no value appears in cell C17 because we are attempting to add two blank cells.

Now change the formula in C14 by editing it to

=$B$14+$C$13

which is interpreted as absolute addressing. Copying this formula into cell C17 calculates the correct result. Highlight cell C17 and observe the cell references in its formula; they have not changed from those of cell C14.

The $ sign must prefix both the column reference and the row reference. Mixed cell addressing is permitted; as for example when a column address reference is needed to be taken as absolute, while a row address reference is needed to be taken as relative. In such a case, the column letter is prefixed by the $ sign.

When building an absolute cell reference in a formula, it is easier to select each cell address within a formula by double-clicking on it with the left mouse button then, when selected, keep on pressing the **F4** key until the correct $ prefix is set.

Freezing Panes on Screen

Sometimes there might be too much information on screen and attempting to see a certain part of a sheet might cause the labels associated with that information to scroll off the screen.

To freeze column (or row) labels of a worksheet on screen, move the cell pointer to the right (or below) the column (or row) which you want to freeze, and use the **Window, Freeze Panes** command. Everything to the left of (or above) the cell pointer will freeze on the screen.

To unfreeze panes, use the **Window, Unfreeze Panes** command.

9

Spreadsheet Charts

Excel allows information within a worksheet to be represented in graphical form, which makes data more accessible to non-expert users who might not be familiar with the spreadsheet format. The saying 'a picture is worth a thousand words', applies equally well to charts and figures.

The package allows the use of several chart and graph types, including area, bar, column, line, doughnut, radar, XY, pie, combination, and several 3-D options of these charts. In all, Excel allows fourteen different types of charts, with almost 100 predefined formats, which can be selected by using the appropriate icon. These are made available to you once you have selected the data you want to chart and clicked on the Chart Wizard button on the toolbar.

Charts (you can have several per worksheet) can be displayed on screen at the same time as the worksheet from which they were derived, since they appear in their own 'chart' frame and can be embedded anywhere on a worksheet. Furthermore, they can be sent to an appropriate output device, such as a plotter or printer. Although this charting module rivals a standalone graphics package, and one could write a separate book on it, an attempt will be made to present its basics, in the space available within this book.

Preparing for a Column Chart

In order to illustrate some of the graphing capabilities of Excel, we will now plot the income of the consulting company we discussed in the **Project 6** file. However, before we can go on, you will need to complete the entries for the last two quarters of trading of the Adept Consultants' example, if you haven't already done so - see end of previous chapter.

Next, link the quarterly totals to the consolidation sheet, calculate the year's total, as shown below, and save the resultant workbook as **Project 7**, before going on.

	A	B	C	D	E	F	G
	F4	▼	= =SUM(B4:E4)				
1		*Project Analysis - Year Summary*					
2							
3		1st Quarter	2nd Quarter	3rd Quarter	4th Quarter	Total	
4	Income	£45,000.00	£48,000.00	£52,500.00	£ 57,000.00	£202,500.00	
5	Costs:						
6	Wages	£ 9,000.00	£12,000.00	£13,500.00	£ 15,000.00	£ 49,500.00	
7	Travel	£ 1,500.00	£ 1,630.00	£ 1,930.00	£ 2,000.00	£ 7,060.00	
8	Rent	£ 900.00	£ 900.00	£ 900.00	£ 900.00	£ 3,600.00	
9	Heat/Light	£ 480.00	£ 370.00	£ 250.00	£ 610.00	£ 1,710.00	
10	Phone/Fax	£ 900.00	£ 1,050.00	£ 1,150.00	£ 1,270.00	£ 4,370.00	
11	Adverts	£ 3,600.00	£ 3,900.00	£ 4,350.00	£ 4,510.00	£ 16,360.00	
12	Total Costs	£16,380.00	£19,850.00	£22,080.00	£ 24,290.00	£ 82,600.00	
13	*Profit*	£28,620.00	£28,150.00	£30,420.00	£ 32,710.00	£119,900.00	
14	*Cumulative*	£28,620.00	£56,770.00	£87,190.00	£ 119,900.00		
15							

Now we need to select the range of the data we want to graph. The range of data to be graphed in Excel does not have to be contiguous for each graph, as with some other spreadsheets. With Excel, you select your data from different parts of a sheet with the <Ctrl> key pressed down. This method has the advantage of automatic recalculation should any changes be made to the original data. You could also collect data from different sheets to one 'graphing' sheet by linking them as we did with the consolidation sheet.

If you don't want the chart to be recalculated when you do this, then you must use the **Edit, Copy** and **Edit, Paste Special** commands and choose the **Values** option from the displayed dialogue box, which copies a selected range to a specified target area of the worksheet and converts formulae to values. This is necessary, as cells containing formulae cannot be pasted directly since it would cause the relative cell addresses to adjust to the new locations; each formula would then recalculate a new value for each cell and give wrong results.

The Chart Wizard

To obtain a chart of 'Income' versus 'Quarters', select the
data in cell range A3..E4, then either click the Chart
Wizard button, shown here, or use the **Insert, Chart**
command. The Chart Wizard then opens the first of
four dialogue boxes, as shown below, which guide
you through the process.

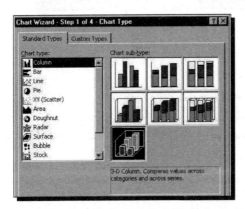

Now select the 3-D Column type and click the **Next >** button
at the bottom of the displayed Chart Wizard dialogue box (not
shown above). The second dialogue box is then displayed as
follows, after clicking the **Columns** radio button pointed to
below.

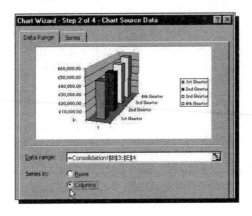

The third Chart Wizard dialogue box allows you to give a title to your chart and annotate the x- and y-axes, while the fourth dialogue box allows you to place the chart either on a separate sheet or on the sheet that was active when you first started the charting process. On pressing the **Finish** button the following chart should appear on your worksheet.

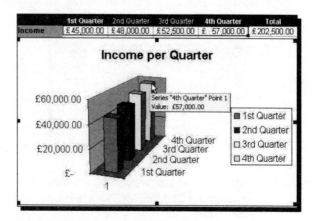

Note that to find out the exact details of a given column on a chart, you need only place the mouse pointer on it to cause a banner to appear with the desired information.

While the frame containing a chart is selected (you can tell from the presence of the small black squares around it), you can change its size by dragging the small two-headed arrow pointer (which appears when the mouse pointer is placed on the small black squares of the frame). You can also move the frame and its contents to another position on the worksheet by pointing to the chart area, pressing and keeping depressed the left mouse button until the pointer changes to a small four-headed arrow shape, then dragging the changed mouse pointer to a new position.

As an example of what you can do with a chart, let us first select it, then either double-click within the chart area or use the **Format, Selected Chart Area** command to obtain the following dialogue box:

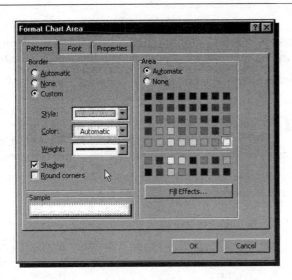

From this dialogue box you can choose a pattern to be used as a frame, by selecting **Custom** under the Patterns tab and choose the 8th **Style**, the 4th **Weight** line, check the **Shadow** box and press **OK**.

Try it, then change the second quarter income from £48,000 to £58,000 (on the Quarter 2 sheet), and watch how the change is reflected on the redrawn graph on the Consolidation sheet displayed below.

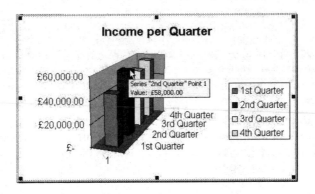

You can change the type of chart shown on screen by first selecting it, then using the **Chart, Chart Type** command to display the first Chart Wizard dialogue box.

Finally, revert to the original entry for the first quarter's income, change your chart back to a simple column type, and then save your work again under the filename **Project 7** by simply pressing the Save icon shown here. Your current work will be saved to disc replacing the previous version under the same filename.

When Excel creates a chart, it plots each row or column of data in the selected range as a 'data series', such as a group of bars, lines, etc. A chart can contain many data series, but Excel charts data according to the following rules:

1.   If the selected range contains more rows than columns of data, Excel plots the data series by columns.

X-axis labels   1st data series   2nd data series   3rd data series

2.   If the selected range contains more columns than rows of data, or the same number of columns and rows, Excel plots the data series by rows.

Legend   X-axis labels
labels   1st data series
             2nd data series

If you select a range to chart which includes column and row headings, and text above or to the left of the numeric data, Excel uses the text to create the axis labels, legends, and title.

If your data selection does not obey these rules, you must tell Excel how your data series is structured in the 2nd Chart Wizard dialogue box.

Editing a Chart

The easiest way to edit a chart is to right-click it while pointing within the chart area, but near its outer rim. This displays the shortcut menu shown here. As a chart is made up of several objects, for example, data series, plot area, the various axis data area, legends, and chart area, you will get a different shortcut menu if you were pointing to these different areas. Try it. As you right-click different areas, their name will appear in the 'Name box' which is situated below the 'Font' box. The shortcut menu shown here is the one you will get when you right-click the 'Chart Area'.

We have already used the first menu option to format our chart. The second menu option allows you to quickly change the chart type, while the third option can be used to change the source data. The fourth menu option allows you to add Titles, change axes, add grid lines and data labels, while the fifth option lets you specify whether you want your chart to be located in a new sheet or where you created it.

Saving Charts

When you save a workbook, the chart or charts you have created are saved with it. It is, therefore, a good idea not only to give each chart a title, but to also locate it on a differently named sheet.

Use the **Chart Options** in the above shortcut menu to give this chart the title **Income per Quarter**, and the **Location** option to put the chart on a separate sheet and give it the name **Income Bar**. Finally, save the workbook under the filename **Project 8**.

Predefined Chart Types

To select a different type of chart, click the Chart Wizard icon

 shown here, or select the **Insert, Chart** command. The 1st Chart Wizard dialogue box displayed previously, lists 14 different chart options. These chart-types are normally used to describe the following relationships between data:

 Area: for showing a volume relationship between two series, such as production or sales, over a given length of time.

 Bar: for comparing differences in data (noncontinuous data that are not related over time) by depicting changes in horizontal bars to show positive and negative variations from a given position.

 Bubble: for showing a type of XY (scatter) chart. The size of the data (radius of the bubble) indicates the value of a third variable.

 Column: for comparing separate items (noncontinuous data which are related over time) by depicting changes in vertical bars to show positive and negative variations from a given position.

 Cone: for showing 3-D column and bar charts in a more dramatic way.

 Cylinder: similar to Cone.

 Doughnut: for comparing parts with the whole. Similar to pie charts, but can depict more than one series of data.

	Line:	for showing continuous changes in data with time.
	Pie:	for comparing parts with the whole. You can use this type of chart when you want to compare the percentage of an item from a single series of data with the whole series.
	Pyramid:	similar to Cone.
	Radar:	for plotting one series of data as angle values defined in radians, against one or more series defined in terms of a radius.
	Surface:	for showing optimum combinations between two sets of data, as in a topographic map. Colours and patterns indicate areas that are in the same range of values.
	Stock:	for showing high-low-close type of data variation to illustrate stock market prices or temperature changes.
	XY (Scatter):	for showing scatter relationships between X and Y. Scatter charts are used to depict items which are not related over time.

You can change the type of chart by selecting one of the fourteen offered when the **Chart Type** button is clicked on the Chart Toolbar. This bar is opened whenever a chart is selected, as follows,

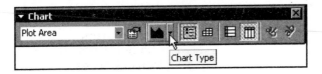

provided you have activated it using the **View**, **Toolbars** command.

Customising a Chart

In order to customise a chart, you need to know how to add legends, titles, text labels, arrows, and how to change the colour and pattern of the chart background, plot areas and chart markers, and how to select, move and size chart objects.

Drawing a Multiple Column Chart

As an exercise, we will consider a new column chart which deals with the quarterly 'Costs' of Adept Consultants. To achieve this, first select the Consolidation sheet of workbook **Project 8**, then highlight the cell range A3:E3, press the <Ctrl> key, and while holding it down, use the mouse to select the costs range A6:E11.

Next, click the Chart Wizard icon (or use the **Insert, Chart** command), select Column from the **Chart type** list, click the fourth **Chart subtype** option, and press the **Next** button. The 6 different quarterly costs will be drawn automatically, as displayed in the composite screen dump below.

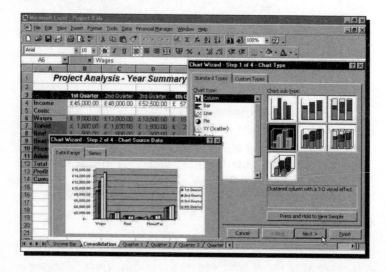

Because the selected range contains more rows than columns of data, Excel follows the 1st rule of data series selection which, however, might not be what you want.

To have the 'quarters' appearing on the x-axis and the 'costs' as the legends, we need to tell Excel that our data series is in rows by clicking the **Rows** button on the 2nd Chart Wizard dialogue box. Immediately this is done the column chart changes to:

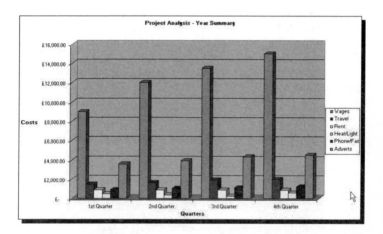

The chart title and axes titles were inserted by typing the heading 'PROJECT ANALYSIS - Year Summary' in the **Chart title** box of the 3rd Chart Wizard dialogue box, followed by the **Axis Titles** shown above.

Once you are satisfied with your efforts, click the **As new sheet** radio button of the 4th Chart Wizard dialogue box, and name your chart **Costs Bar**. If you make a mistake and you want to try again, make sure the unwanted chart is selected, then press the <Del> key. Finally, save your work under the filename **Project 9**.

Changing a Title and an Axis Label

To change a title, an axis label, or a legend within a chart, click the appropriate area on the chart. This reveals that these are individual objects (they are surrounded by small black squares) and you can edit, reposition them, or change their font and point size. You can even rotate text within such areas in any direction you like.

To demonstrate these options, we will use the **Costs Bar** chart saved in **Project 9**, so get it on screen if you are to follow our suggestions.

To change the font size of a chart title, click the Chart Title area to select it and double-click on the border that is displayed when you select such an object. Doing this, displays the Format dialogue box for the selected object, and clicking the Font tab reveals the following:

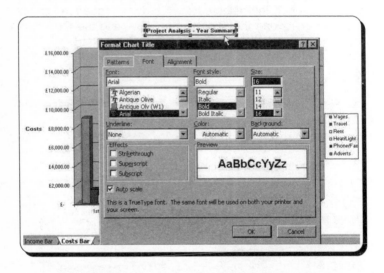

From here, we changed the font size of the chart title from 12 to 16 points. We also selected the Costs label and changed its size from 10 to 14 points, then clicked the Alignment tab to change its orientation to 90°, as shown on the next page.

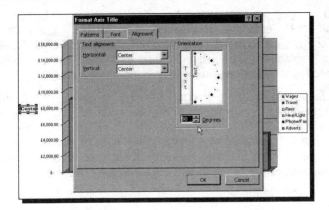

Drawing a Pie Chart

To change the chart type, simply select the chart, then click the Chart Wizard and choose the 3-D Pie chart from the displayed list. If the selected chart was the 'quarterly costs' chart, then clicking the **Next** button, checking the **Columns** radio button and clicking **Next**, displays the chart type that would be redrawn for the specified data series, as shown below.

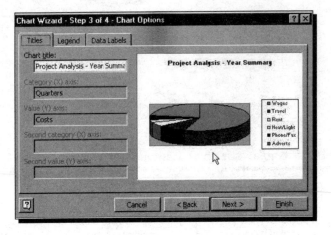

However, so as not to spoil your **Costs Bar** chart, click the **Cancel** button at this stage.

To obtain a pie chart without spoiling the chart it is based on, you must select the data range again, then click the Chart Wizard, choose the pie chart from the displayed chart types, then select the specific pie chart that best fits your data, specify the type of series, and give the chart a title.

As a last example in chart drawing, we will use the data range A6:A11 and F6:F11 of the Consolidation worksheet to plot a 3-D pie chart. The steps are the same as before, but for the 3-D option and specifying the type of series data as 'columns'. Note that the chart title should now reflect the Year Totals, rather than the Quarter summaries. The result should be as follows:

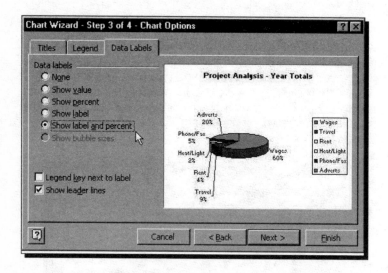

To display the above chart, we clicked the Data Labels tab and the **Show label and percent** radio button in the 3rd dialogue box of the Chart Wizard.

This chart tells us, for example, that Wages for the whole year amount to 60% of the total yearly costs. Other cost categories are also displayed with their appropriate percentages. Clicking the **Finish** button displays the pie chart in its finished form, as shown overleaf.

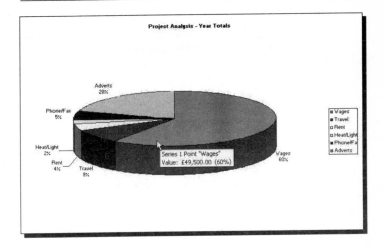

Pointing to any pie slice, causes the pop-up poster to be displayed, informing you of the actual data series, its value and its percentage of the whole. It is now obvious that the information contained in this chart is much more than in the 2-D version.

If you want to explode an individual pie slice, you can do so by simply dragging it. This is possible as each slice is treated as a separate object, but you must increase the size of your chart before you can accurately pinpoint the required slice.

Finally, use the **Chart, Location** menu command to name this last version of the pie chart as **Costs Pie** and save your workbook.

* * *

Excel has many more features than the ones we have introduced in this book. For example, you could use Excel's database and macro capabilities, and also explore its various tools, such as the Goal Seek, Scenarios, Auditing, and Solver. We hope we have given you sufficient basic knowledge to be able to explore these topics by yourself.

However, if you would prefer to be guided through these topics, then may we suggest you look up the later chapters of the book   *Microsoft Excel 2000 explained* (BP473), also published by BERNARD BABANI (publishing) Ltd.

* * *

10

The PowerPoint Environment

Microsoft PowerPoint 2000 is a powerful and versatile Graphics Presentation package which deserves more attention than it gets from most users of Microsoft Office.

The key element of PowerPoint is the Slide Show and the production of ancillary material, such as scripted notes to accompany each slide, laser copies of slides, and an outline view of all the information in the presentation. However, Microsoft uses the word slide to refer to each individual page of a presentation and you can format the output for overhead projector acetates, or electronic presentation on screen.

In addition, you can apply the skills you have already gained in using Word and Excel and use material created in these applications within PowerPoint.

Starting the PowerPoint Program

PowerPoint is started in Windows either by clicking the **Start** button then selecting **Programs** and clicking on the

 'Microsoft PowerPoint' icon on the cascade menu, clicking the PowerPoint button on the Office Shortcut Bar, or by clicking the 'Open a Document' button on the Office Shortcut Bar and double-clicking on a PowerPoint presentation file. In the latter case the presentation will be loaded into PowerPoint at the same time.

 The first time you use PowerPoint, it might be a good idea to activate the Assistant and type 'What's new' in the text box, then click **Search**.

This causes the Help screen to the left to be displayed. Clicking the 'What's new in PowerPoint 2000' menu option, opens up a Help dialogue box with the same name, as shown below.

We suggest you spend a little time here browsing through the various help screens. After doing so, click the **Help Topics** button at the top left of the dialogue box to display more information on PowerPoint 2000.

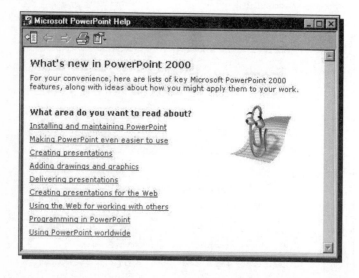

There are even more help topics, including 'Key information' hidden away within the Help System. To reach these topics, click the Show button at the top left corner of the above Help screen which opens a list of help books which you can open to reach a wealth of extra information on PowerPoint. Try it!

The PowerPoint Screen

When PowerPoint is loaded, a screen displays with similar Title bar, Menu bar, Toolbar and Formatting bar to those of Word and Excel. Obviously there are differences, but that is to be expected as PowerPoint serves a different purpose to the other programs.

The opening screen of PowerPoint is shown below. The program follows the usual Microsoft Windows conventions with which you should be very familiar by now. Scroll bars and scroll buttons only appear within the window in which you load a presentation.

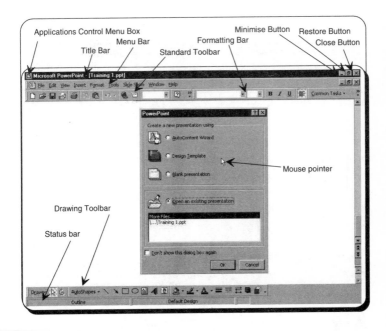

In the middle of the opening screen, the PowerPoint dialogue box is displayed. The options in this dialogue box make it easy for you to start your presentation.

These options allow you to create a new presentation, as follows:

AutoContent Wizard

> Activates a Wizard that helps you determine the content and organisation of your presentation.

Design Template

> Allows you to select a presentation template that determines the colour scheme, fonts, and other design features of the presentation.

Blank Presentation

> Allows you to start with a blank presentation with all values for colour scheme, fonts, and other design features set to default values. The same dialogue box also displays when you click the New button on the Standard Toolbar.

The last option, at the bottom of the PowerPoint dialogue box, allows you to **Open an existing presentation**. Clicking this option, displays the File Open dialogue box which also displays when you click the Open button on the Standard Toolbar.

From the Open dialogue box, you can select where to look

for presentation files, or use the **Tools, Find** menu command, as shown to the left, name a given presentation file in the displayed Find dialogue box, and let the program find it for you.

We will now look for an existing presentation by using the Find dialogue box, so that we can discuss what appears on your screen when a presentation file is opened. First, you will need to click the **New Search** button, then type in the **Value** box the word *Reporting*, as shown below, and change the **Look in** drive to the one into which Office 2000 was installed on your computer. Next, click the **Search sub-folders** box so that it's checked, and press **Find Now** button.

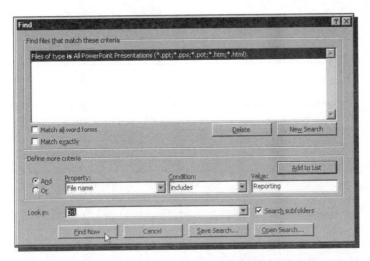

PowerPoint will then ask you to confirm that you want to add the 'File name' property search criteria before closing the Find dialogue box, as shown below. If the Office Assistant is active, the same message will appear on the screen, but on a yellow banner.

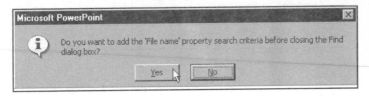

The answer to this message is **Yes** which causes the display of the following dialogue box:

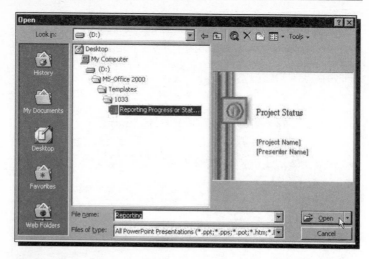

Clicking the **Open** button displays the *Reporting Progress or Status.pot* file.

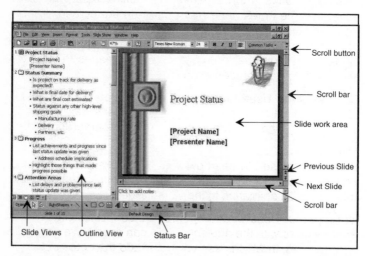

Note the information given on the Status Bar at the bottom of the screen. In this particular case it tells you that you are looking at the first of ten slides using the Default Design.

PowerPoint Views

The Slide Views bar at the bottom left corner of the Presentation window, is shown enlarged below.

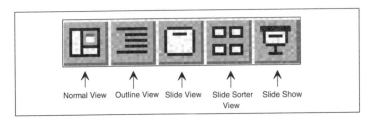

These five Slide View buttons are the key to the editing power of PowerPoint.

Normal View

This view contains three panes: the outline pane, the slide pane, and the notes pane (not shown on the screen dump). You can adjust the size of the different panes by dragging the pane borders; one way of revealing the notes pane, the other by using the scroll bar. You can use these panes to work on all aspects of your presentation.

Outline pane: Used to organise and develop the content of your presentation. You can type all of the text of your presentation and rearrange bullet points, paragraphs, and slides.

Slide pane: Used to see how your text looks on each slide. You can add graphics, videos, and sounds, create hyper links, and add animation to individual slides.

Notes pane: Used to add speaker notes or information you want to share with the audience. You can even have graphics in your notes, in which case you must add the notes in Notes Page View - use the **View, Notes Page** menu command.

These three panes are also displayed when you save your presentation as a Web page. The only difference is that the outline pane displays a table of contents so that you can navigate through your presentation.

Outline View

In this view, the Outline View pane is enlarged making it easier for you to organise and edit your presentation text. The notes pane is also visible, allowing you to add speaker's notes as you go along.

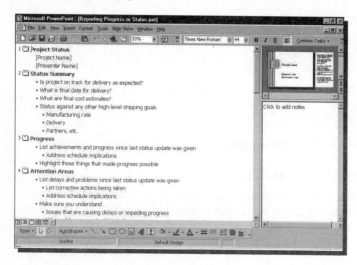

Slide View

The Slide View allows you to see an enlarged slide area of a selected slide. To select another slide, click on the column of numbered slides making up your presentation.

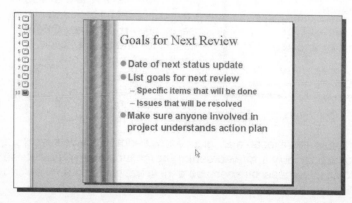

Slide Sorter View

In this view, you can see the whole presentation at once. You can reorder slides, add transitions, and set timing for electronic presentations. You can also select animated transitions for moving from slide to slide.

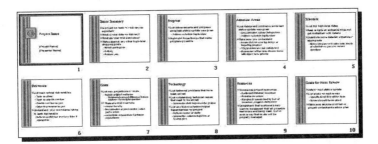

Notes Pages View

This is where you create speaker's notes which contain graphics for any or all of your presentation slides. To open up this view, use the **View, Notes Page** menu command.

As an example, we have used the 10th slide from our demonstration set, and imported a graphic in the speaker's notes area, as shown to the left. To do this, first type a line of text, similar to 'This is a test to see if a picture could be included', then use the **Insert, Picture, Clip Art** menu command (or click the Insert Clip Art button on the Draw Toolbar instead), and select an appropriate graphic (we will discuss this procedure in detail in the next chapter).

Drawing objects and pictures are not displayed in the notes pane (try it for yourself), but appear when you work in Notes Page View or when you print slides with notes.

Slide Show View

In this view you see your work as an electronic presentation, with each slide filling the screen. You can also see the effect of the transitions and timing that you set in the Slide Sorter View.

To see the next slide in full-screen view either click the left mouse button or press the right cursor key. To return to a

previous slide in full-screen view press the left cursor key. To return to a previous PowerPoint view from a full-screen Slide Show View, press <Esc>, or click the right mouse button to display the quick menu, shown here, and click the **End Show** menu option.

The fourth and fifth menu options can be used in the following way:

While you are showing a slide show, you can take minutes, record action items, and add to your notes pages by right-clicking a slide while in full-view and selecting the **Meeting Minder** menu option which opens the dialogue box shown below.

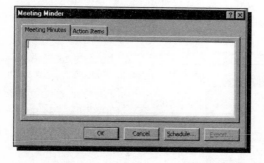

Such notes only appear on your screen - other participants see only the slide show. Action items appear on a new slide at the end of your slide show and can be posted to Microsoft Outlook, or can be transferred to a new Word document and then printed with that document.

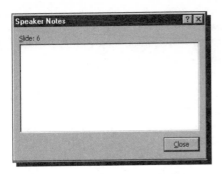

While preparing a presentation, you can make notes relating to each slide by right-clicking a slide while in full-screen view and selecting the **Speaker Notes** menu option. This displays the dialogue box shown to the left.

These notes can be printed and then used either to remember key points during a presentation, or to help the audience follow the presentation. Both the notes and handout pages have masters, where you can add items you want to appear on each page.

Setting Transition, Animation and Timings

Your presentation will appear more professional if you set timings, transition and animation. To do this, activate the Slide Sorter View and observe the extra Toolbar that appears below the Standard and Formatting Bars.

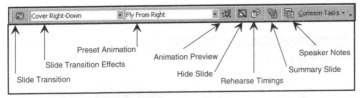

Clicking the first button on Slide Sorter Toolbar, displays the Slide Transition dialogue box, shown here. You can select a Transition Effect by clicking the down-arrow below the graphic and choosing one from the drop-down list, then left-click the mouse on the graphic to see its effect.

You can select a different Slide Transition Effect and Preset Animation for each selected slide. Having done so, select a slide and click the Animation Preview button on the Toolbar to see its effect.

You can set timings for a slide show by either clicking the Rehearse Timings button on the Toolbar, or using the **Sli̲de Show, ̲Rehearse Timings** menu command, to start a slide show from a selected slide onwards and simultaneously display the Rehearse dialogue box at the top left of the screen.

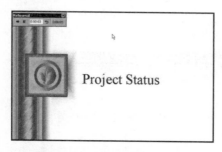

As you can see from our screen dump, only the first title appears on the screen. The time it takes you to click the large left arrow on the Rehearse dialogue box, shown enlarged

to the right, is the actual time it will take for the fist subtitle to appear on this first slide. Once all the

information has been added to this slide, clicking the left arrow displays the next slide in the sequence, and so on.

When you stop the Slide Show View, PowerPoint displays the following dialogue box:

Pressing **̲Yes** records the slide timings and uses them next time you select the Slide Show View, but if they do not suit you, they can be changed by restarting the whole process. The current effective timings are displayed below each slide, as shown below, when in Slide Sorter View.

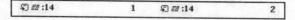

The Slide Master

While a slide is selected, you can get a lot of help from the Assistant if you do the following:

- Click on the Assistant to open the 'What would you like to do?' help box, type the string 'slide master', and click the **S**earch button.

- In the displayed dialogue box, select the first option 'The slide master' and click the **S**earch button.

This opens up an extremely useful help screen, shown below, from which you can learn a lot.

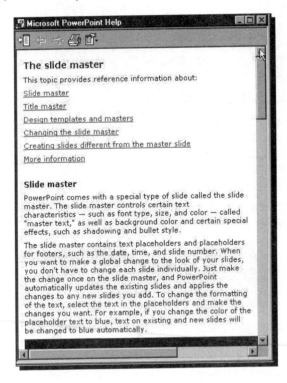

In essence, each design template comes with its own slide master. The elements on the slide master control the design of the template, many of which have a separate title master.

When you apply a design template to a presentation, PowerPoint automatically updates the text styles and graphics on the slide master (one of which is shown below), and changes the colour scheme to the one in the new design template. Any object you have added to the slide master, such as a text box or graphic, will not be deleted when you apply a new design template.

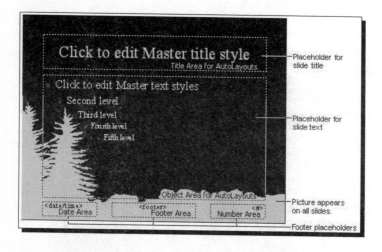

Even though we will be covering in the next chapter most of the points raised in the above help screen, it will be a good idea if you spend some time with it.

11

Designing a Presentation

In this chapter we will use PowerPoint's Wizards to design a simple presentation quickly and effectively. Below, we show the first page of the finished presentation in overhead format, so that you can have an idea of the overall design.

The AutoContent Wizard

When you first start PowerPoint, you are offered the opportunity to use the Wizard, select a template on which to base your work, begin with a blank presentation, or open an existing presentation.

Most users would, without question, like to produce a presentation in no time at all. The **AutoContent Wizard** is an excellent starting point, even if you know what you want to do and how to do it.

Later you can customise your presentation using
PowerPoint's editing tools. But for now, select the
AutoContent Wizard and click the **OK** button, to start the
display of five dialogue boxes in which you are:

- Provided with ideas and an organisation for your
  presentation.

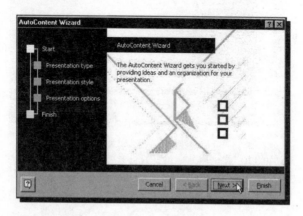

- Asked to select the type of presentation you are going
  to give (we selected *Training*).

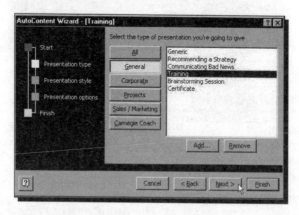

- Asked to specify what type of output you require (we selected *Black and white overheads*).

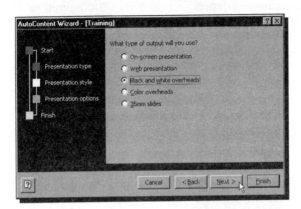

- Asked to type in the title of your presentation (we typed *PowerPoint Wizard*, and deleted the contents of **Additional information**).

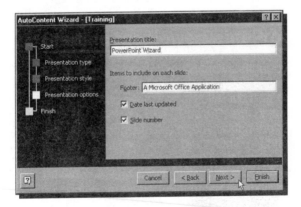

- Told that this is the only information required to create your presentation.

Clicking the **Finish** button on the last dialogue box, creates your presentation and displays it in Outline mode complete with suggested topics. These can be changed to suit your needs, as shown below, where the 3rd slide is displayed.

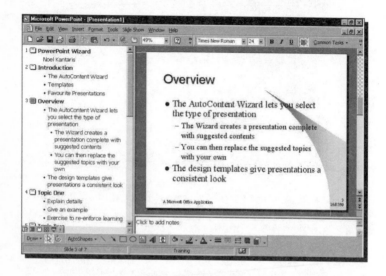

In this slide, we have added some extra demoted (more indented) topics by using the <Tab> key, and deleted topics that were of no relevance to our presentation. To return to the original bullet level from a demoted level, use the <Shift+Tab> key.

Text could be demoted or promoted using the Demote and Promote buttons, shown here and to be found on the Formatted Bar. To use these you must either select them from the **More Buttons** drop-down menu of the Formatting Bar, or move this Toolbar and place it below the Standard Toolbar, which reveals the extra buttons automatically. The result of our efforts can be displayed on screen, as shown on the next page, by clicking the Slide View button at the bottom of the screen.

The actual name of the person designing these slides that appears below the title, is taken by PowerPoint automatically from information held on the *user* of the program. You could replace this by editing the relevant line when in Outline View.

Save the result of your work so far under the filename **Training 1**.

Clicking the Slide Sorter View button at the bottom of the screen, displays all the slides in your presentation, as follows:

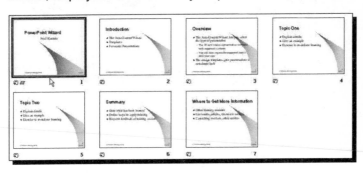

To move a slide to a different position in the set, simply left-click it and drag the modified pointer to the new position.

Selecting a Template

Our presentation might not look exactly what we had in mind, but we can select a different template to change the overall design. To change the default design of slides, first click the Slide Sorter View button, then do the following:

* Double-click the area at the bottom of the screen on the Status bar that holds the name of the current template (in our example this should read **Training**). This opens the Apply Design Template dialogue box, shown below, with the Presentation Designs folder in the **Look in** box. This folder is within the Templates folder of PowerPoint.

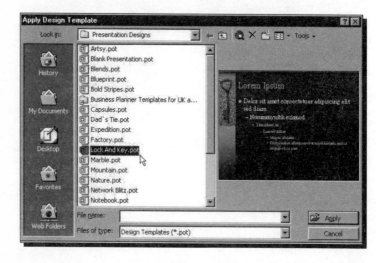

* Select the **Lock And Key.pot** design, and click the **Apply** button.

What appears on your screen next, is the display on the next page, shown in black and white format. Note the column of slide icons to the left of the screen. As you click one of these icons, its corresponding slide is displayed in full size.

Adding a Drawing to a Presentation

You can use the various buttons on the Drawing Toolbar at the bottom of the screen (if not activated use the **View, Toolbars, Drawing** command) to add to your presentation. The function of each Drawing tool is described on the next page.

To use the various Drawing tools, you must have a Presentation window open (we chose the second slide of our Training example), and if you want your drawing to occur in all subsequent slides, then you should use the **View, Master, Slide Master** menu command and start your drawing on the displayed Master slide, otherwise it will only appear on the slide you have selected.

Below, we used the Oval tool, the Text Box tool, and the Fill Colour tool to produce the logo shown here, which we placed at the bottom left corner of our presentation, as shown overleaf.

You, of course, can use your drawing skills to produce your own logo. Save your creation under **Training 2**.

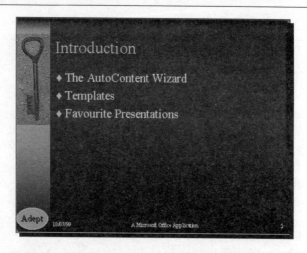

The buttons on the Drawing Toolbar have the following functions and are described on the next page.

Group objects, etc.

Select Objects

Free Rotate

Select from various shapes

Line

Arrow

Rectangle

Oval

Text Box

Insert WordArt

Insert Clip Art

Fill Colour

Shadow

3-D

More Buttons

The Drawing Toolbar

The various functions offered by the Drawing Toolbar are shared by all Office 2000 applications and give PowerPoint a superior graphics capability. Amongst the many features available are:

AutoShapes – the additional AutoShape categories, such as connectors, block arrows, flowchart symbols, stars and banners, callouts, and action buttons make drawing diagrams much easier.

Bezier curves – used to easily create exact curves with pinpoint precision.

3-D effects – allow you to transform 2-D shapes into realistic 3-D objects with new 3-D effects, such as changing the lighting perspective of a 3-D object.

Perspective shadows – allow you to select from a wide range of shadows with perspective, and you can adjust the depth and angle of each shadow to make pictures more realistic.

Connectors – used to create diagrams and flowcharts with new straight, angled, and curved connectors between the shapes; when shapes are moved, the connectors remain attached and automatically reposition themselves.

Arrowhead styles – allow you to change the width and height of arrowheads for maximum effect.

Object alignment – allow you to distribute and space objects evenly, both horizontally and vertically.

Precise line-width control – allows you increased control over the width of lines by selecting pre-set options or customised line widths.

Image editing – lets you easily adjust the brightness or contrast of a picture.

Transparent background – allows you to insert a bit map on your slides or Web pages so as to appear to be part of the design by turning background colours into transparent areas.

Inserting a Clip Art Image

To personalise our work, let us insert a clip art image on the

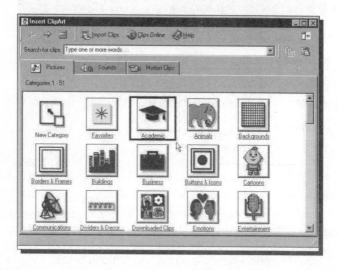

front page of our presentation. To do this, click the Insert Clip Art button, shown here, on the Drawing Toolbar. This opens the Microsoft Clip Art Gallery, from which you can choose a picture.

Usually, most of the Clip Art Gallery is held on one of the Office distribution CD-ROM discs because of its size. Note the different categories; there are 50 in all, each one of which has between 25 to 100 images. We chose the first image of the first row of the Academic category, called 'activities'.

When you click on a graphic, the drop-down menu shown here is displayed, and clicking the **Insert clip** button, transfers the image onto the title page of our presentation (provided it was selected).

Our final result (we will tell you what text enhancements to apply), is on the next page, but as you can see the graphic is not in the ideal position.

Rearranging Items on a Slide

All items on a presentation slide, including parts of the template design, can be moved to a different position. To do this on the title (1st) slide of your presentation, use the **View, Master, Title Master** menu command, while to move something on all the rest of the slides, use the **View, Master, Slide Master** menu command and follow the instructions we discuss below.

If, on the other hand, you wanted to move an item on a specific slide only (other than one that is part of the template), then display the slide in question in either Normal or Slide View and follow the same instructions below.

On the next page, we show the process of moving the main title from its present position to a new position slightly above than its current position, as shown by the dotted rectangle. To achieve this, do the following:

- Point within the text area of the title and when the mouse pointer changes to an insertion bar, click the left mouse button. This causes a border to appear around the title with small handles on it, which can be used to increase or decrease the size of the border.

- To move the title, place the mouse pointer on the title border and when the mouse pointer changes to four small arrows in the shape of a cross, drag the border to its new position.

To obtain the design shown on the next page, do the following:

- Move the name of the presentation author to the bottom left corner of the presentation, reduce the border around it, then select the name by clicking on it and reduce the font size to 24. This helps to reduce the prominence of the author's name on the slide, and allows a large enough space to be created in the middle of the slide for the enlargement of the Clip Art object.

- Select the title and click the Text Box tool to allow you to add the words 'One step at a time' below the main title, set its font size to 28 and centre it below the title.

- Move the inserted Clip Art graphic to its new position and enlarge it as shown.

Save the final presentation as **Training 3**. PowerPoint inserts the three letter extension **.ppt**, to distinguish such files from others in the Office suite. In the future, double-clicking on this file in a My Computer or Explorer window, will open PowerPoint with the file active.

As an exercise, try to change the template of our presentation to that of 'Strategic', and change the first slide of it to the following:

The Picture Bar

Should you want to change a picture you have inserted into your presentation, use the **View, Toolbars** command and select **Picture** from the drop-down menu. The tools on this bar can be used to manipulate pictures to suit your needs. Their functions are as follows:

Insert Picture from File

Image Control

More Contrast

Less Contrast

More Brightness

Less Brightness

Crop

Line Style

Recolor Picture

Format Picture

Set Transparent Color

Reset Picture

Try using these tools on an imported image to see how you can enhance or utterly destroy it! If, at the end of the day, you don't save it, it doesn't matter what you do to it. Just experiment.

* * *

PowerPoint is obviously capable of a lot more than we have introduced here, but you should now have the confidence to explore more of the package by yourself.

12

The Access Database

Microsoft Access is a database management system (DBMS) designed to allow users to store, manipulate and retrieve information easily and quickly. A database is a collection of data that exists and is organised around a specific theme or requirement. It can be of the 'flat-file' type, or it can have relational capabilities, as in the case of Access, which is known as a relational database management system (RDBMS).

The main difference between flat-file and relational database systems is that the latter can store and manipulate data in multiple 'tables', while the former systems can only manipulate a single table at any given time. To make accessing the data easier, each row (or **record**) of data within a database table is structured in the same fashion, i.e., each record will have the same number of columns (or **fields**).

We define a database and its various elements as:

Database	A collection of data organised for a specific theme in one or more tables.
Table	A two-dimensional structure in which data is stored, like in a spreadsheet
Record	A row of information in a table relating to a single entry and comprising one or more fields.
Field	A single column of information of the same type, such as people's names.

In Access 2000 the maximum size of a database is 2 gigabytes and in addition it can include linked tables in other files. The number of objects in a database is limited to 32,768, while the maximum number of fields in a table is 255.

A good example of a flat-file database is the invoicing details kept on clients by a company. These details could include name of client, description of work done, invoice number, and amount charged, as follows:

NAME	Consultancy	Invoice	Value
VORTEX Co. Ltd	Wind Tunnel Tests	9901	120.84
AVON Construction	Adhesive Tests	9902	103.52
BARROWS Associates	Tunnel Design Tests	9903	99.32
STONEAGE Ltd	Carbon Dating Tests	9904	55.98
PARKWAY Gravel	Material Size Tests	9905	180.22
WESTWOOD Ltd	Load Bearing Tests	9906	68.52

Such a flat-file DBMS is too limited for the type of information normally held by most companies. If the same client asks for work to be carried out regularly, then the details for that client (which could include address, telephone and fax numbers, contact name, date of invoice, etc.), will have to be entered several times. This can lead to errors, but above all to redundant information being kept on a client - each entry will have to have the name of the client, their address, telephone and fax numbers.

The relational facilities offered by Access, overcome the problems of entry errors and duplication of information. The ability to handle multiple tables at any one time allows for the grouping of data into sensible subsets. For example, one table, called client, could hold the names of the clients, their addresses, telephone and fax numbers, while another table, called invoice, could hold information on the work done, invoice number, date of issue, and amount charged. The two tables must have one unique common field, such as a client reference number. The advantage is that details of each client are entered and stored only once, thus reducing the time and effort wasted on entering duplicate information, and also reducing the space required for data storage.

Starting the Access Program

Access is started in Windows either by clicking the **Start** button then selecting **P̲rograms** and clicking on the

'Microsoft Access' icon on the cascade menu, clicking the Access button or the 'Open Office Document' icon on the Office Shortcut Bar, or by clicking and double-clicking on an Access database file. In the latter case the document will be loaded into Access at the same time.

When you start the Access program by either of the first two methods, the following dialogue box is displayed in the middle of your screen:

From here, you can either create a new database, or **Open an existing file**. If you elect to create a new database, then you can select either to create a **B̲lank Access database**, or use the **A̲ccess database wizards ...** to help you with the creation of the new database. Access 2000 makes extensive use of Wizards, which have been designed to help the new user to create databases more easily. In particular, the Database Wizard builds the necessary elements for several different databases for both home and business use. All you have to do is to answer a set of questions and the Wizard builds the database for you.

Parts of the Access Screen

Before we start designing a database, let us take a look at the Access opening screen. Below we also show what displays if you select the **Access database wizards** option.

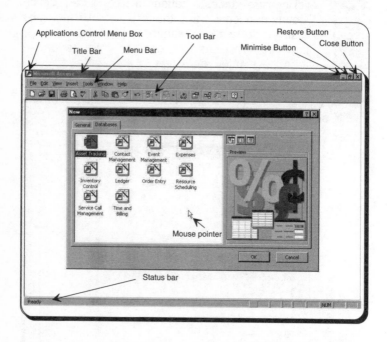

As you can see, these windows have common screen elements with those of other Microsoft Office applications. As usual, depending on what you are doing with Access, the items on the menu bar can be different from those of the opening screen. For example, once a database table is opened the menu bar changes to the following:

Using Help in Access

The first time you start Access, it might be a good idea to look at the help available to you. To do this, cancel the opening dialogue box, then select the **Help, Microsoft Access Help** command which causes a Help screen to be displayed. Below, we only show the left pane of this help screen, so that you can actually read it.

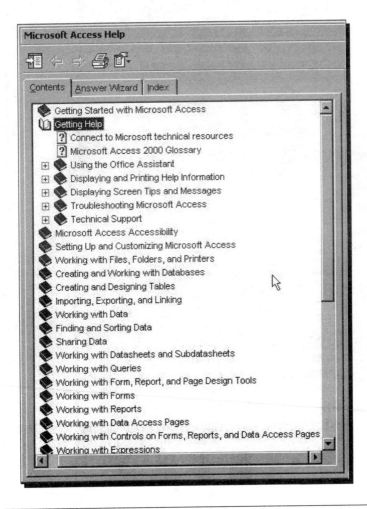

We suggest you spend a little time here browsing through the
various help 'books', particularly the first two; 'Getting Started
with Microsoft Access', and 'Getting Help'. Having done so,
look up the 'Creating and Working with Databases' book
which includes several topics, as shown below.

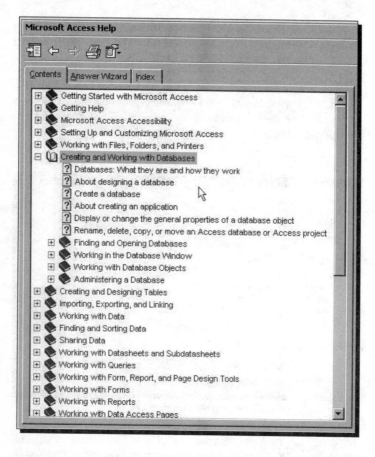

As you can see, there is a wealth of information here, that
you should spend some time going through. Although we will
be introducing most of the topics in this last help book,
getting an additional perspective on the subject can only help
to strengthen the learning process.

Database Elements

Before we start designing a database using Microsoft Access, it will be a good idea if we looked at the various elements that make up a database. To do so, start Access, which opens the Microsoft Access dialogue box.

Next, and if this is being done immediately after starting Access, select the **Access database wizards, pages, and projects** option and click **OK**. Otherwise, either click the New icon on the Standard Toolbar, shown to the left, or use the **File, New** command. Any one of these three methods will cause the New dialogue box to be displayed, as shown below, provided the General tab is the active dialogue box tab at the time.

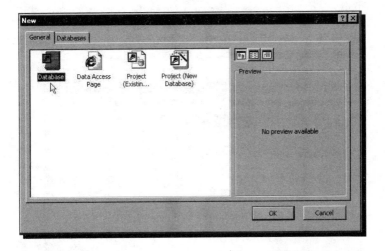

To create a new database, select the Database icon, and press the **OK** button. This opens the File New Database dialogue box shown on the next page.

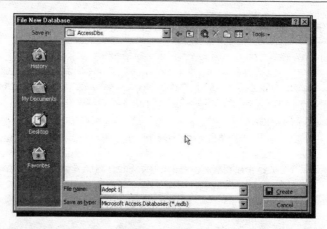

In the **File name** box, type the database name, say **Adept 1**, which replaces the default name **db1**. Access adds the extension **.mdb** automatically. We also decided to save this example in a folder called AccessDbs which was created inside the **My Documents** folder. Finally, pressing the **Create** button displays the Database dialogue box as follows:

It is from here that you can design the various elements that make up a database, such as Tables, Queries, Forms, and Reports, all of which we will examine in some detail in this and the next chapter.

Creating a Table

To design a database table, select Tables from the **Objects** list and click one of the three table-creation icons displayed on the Database dialogue box. We will choose to use the second icon, which opens the Table Wizard with the option of selecting one of two predefined table applications, Business or Personal, as shown below.

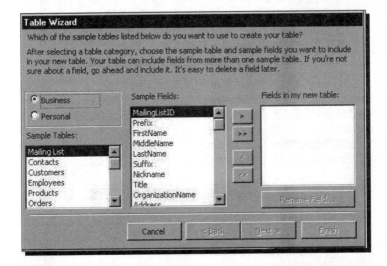

 The same dialogue box can be opened by clicking the **New** button on the Database dialogue box which opens the New Table dialogue box shown to the left. The third option starts the Table Wizard, while the penultimate option allows you to import tables and objects from an external file into the current database, and the last option allows you to link a table in the current database to external tables.

The database we are going to create holds the invoicing details which the firm Adept Consultants keep on their clients. One table will hold the details of the clients, while another will hold the actual invoice details. Therefore, to start, choose 'Customers' from the **Sample Tables** list of the Table Wizard dialogue box, to reveal a list of appropriate fields for that table, as shown below.

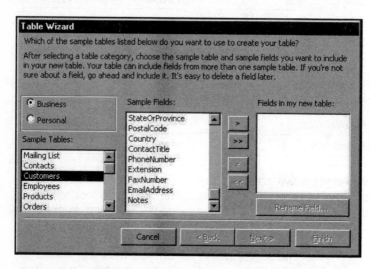

You can either select all the fields or you can select a few. For our example, we selected the following fields: CustomerID, CompanyName, BillingAddress, City, StateOrProvince, PostalCode, ContactTitle, PhoneNumber, FaxNumber and Notes, by highlighting each in turn and pressing the ▸ button.

Don't worry if these field names are not exactly what you want, as they can be easily changed. To change field names, highlight them in turn in the 'Fields in my new table' list and click the **Rename Field** button to reveal the Rename field dialogue box shown here.

We suggest you change the selected field names to those listed below.

CustomerID	CustomerID
CompanyName	Name
BillingAddress	Address
City	Town
StateOrProvince	County
PostalCode	PostCode
ContactTitle	Contact
PhoneNumber	Phone
FaxNumber	Fax
Notes	Order

When you have completed renaming the field names, press the **Next** button, which displays the next of a total of three dialogue boxes. In each of these, do the following, in order of appearance.

* In answer to the question 'Do you want the wizard to set a primary key for you?', click the **No, I'll set the primary key** radio button and press **Next**.

* In answer to the question 'What type of data do you want the primary key field to contain?', click the **Numbers and/or letters I enter when I add new records** radio button and press **Next**.

* In answer to the question 'After the wizard creates the table, what do you want to do?', click the **Enter data directly into the table** radio button, and press **Finish**.

This displays the Customers table, as shown below, ready for you to enter data.

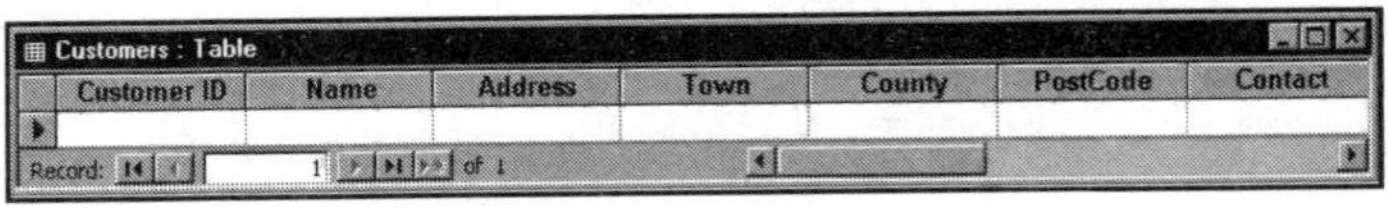

To redesign the table, including changing its field names,

click the Design View icon shown here, or use the **View, Design View** command. The following Table is displayed.

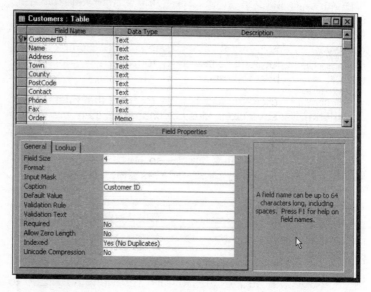

As each field name is highlighted, a Field Properties box appears at the bottom of the screen. If you were using this Table View to rename fields, then you should also edit the name appearing against the Caption property, or remove it altogether.

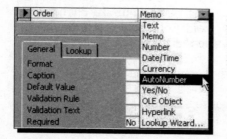

Next, place the cursor at the end of the Data Type descriptor of the Order field which causes a down-arrow button to be displayed. Clicking this button, displays a drop-down list of data types, as shown here.

As the Order field was renamed from one called Notes, Access expects entries in this field to be text by default. However, we intend to use this field as an auto-numbering field, keeping track of the order in which records were added to the database. Hence, we must change the current data type to AutoNumber. Next, place the cursor against the Phone and Fax fields and delete the entry against the Input Mask in the Field Properties box. The type of input mask displayed here is ideal for USA Phone and Fax numbers, but it does not correspond to the entry form usually adopted in the UK, so it is best removed.

Finally, first click the Save icon (or use the **File, Save** command) to save your design changes, then click the Datasheet View button (or use the **View, Datasheet View** command) to revert to the Customers table so that you can start entering information, as shown below.

Customer ID	Name	Address	Town	County	Post Code	Contact
VORT	VORTEX Co. Ltd	Windy House	St. Austell	Cornwall	TR18 1FX	Brian Storm
AVON	AVON Construction	Riverside House	Stratford-on-Avon	Warwickshire	AV15 2QW	John Waters
BARR	BARROWS Associates	Barrows House	Bodmin	Cornwall	PL22 1XE	Mandy Brown
STON	STONEAGE Ltd	Data House	Salisbury	Wiltshire	SB44 1BN	Mike Irons
PARK	PARKWAY Gravel	Aggregate House	Bristol	Avon	BS55 2ZX	James Stone
WEST	WESTWOOD Ltd	Weight House	Plymouth	Devon	PL22 1AA	Mary Slim
GLOW	GLOWORM Ltd	Light House	Brighton	Sussex	BR87 4DD	Peter Summers
SILV	SILVERSMITH Co	Radiation House	Exeter	Devon	EX28 1PL	Adam Smith
WORM	WORMGLAZE Ltd	Glass House	Winchester	Hampshire	WN23 5TR	Richard Glazer
EALI	EALING Engines Design	Engine House	Taunton	Somerset	TN17 3RT	Trevor Miles
HIRE	HIRE Service Equipment	Network House	Bath	Avon	BA76 3WE	Nicole Webb
EURO	EUROBASE Co. Ltd	Control House	Penzance	Cornwall	TR15 8LK	Sarah Star

The widths of the above fields were changed so that all fields could be visible on the screen at the same time. To change the width of a field, place the cursor on the column separator until the cursor changes to the vertical split arrow, then drag the column separator to the right or left, to increase or decrease the width of the field.

Customer ID	Name
VORT	VORTEX Co. Ltd
AVON	AVON Construction
BARR	BARROWS Associates
STON	STONEAGE Ltd

Sorting a Database Table

As you enter information into a database table, you might elect to change the field headings by clicking the Design View icon and editing a field name, say from Name to CompanyName. If you do this, on return to the Customers table you will find that the records have sorted automatically in ascending order of the entries of the field in which you left the cursor while in the Design Table.

If you want to preserve the order in which you entered your data, then sort by the last field (Order) with its type as AutoNumber. This can be done at any time, even after you finished entering all other information in your table.

Sorting a database table in ascending order of an AutoNumber type field, results in the database table displaying in the order in which the data was originally entered in that table. Above, we show the Contact field, so that you can cross-check the original order of your Customer table, as well as the rest of the information in that table not shown in the screen dump of the previous page.

To sort a database table in ascending or descending order

of the entries of any field, place the cursor in the required field and click the Sort Ascending or Sort Descending icon, shown here.

With the keyboard, select the **Records, Sort** command, then choose either the **Sort Ascending** or the **Sort Descending** option.

Applying a Filter to a Sort

If you would like to sort and display only records that fit selected criteria, use the **Records, Filter, Advanced Filter/Sort** command, which opens the Filter dialogue box, shown below.

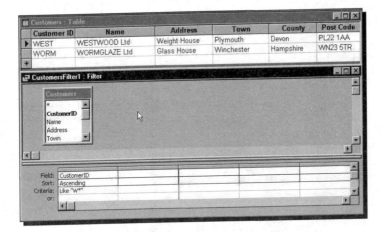

The upper portion of the dialogue box displays all the fields in the Customers table, while the lower portion is where you enter your filter restrictions. In the above example, we chose to view, in ascending order, the records within the CustomerID field that start with W - we typed W* and Access displayed *Like "W*"*.

On pressing the Apply Filter button on the Standard Toolbar, the Customers table displays with only two entries, as seen in the above composite screen dump in which the filter restrictions as well as the result arising from such a filter are displayed. To revert to the display of all the records, click the same icon again, which now appears on the Toolbar depressed, and bears the name Remove Filter.

Using a Database Form

Once a table has been selected from the Database window, clicking the down-arrow against the New Object button and selecting **AutoForm**, automatically displays each record of that table in form view. The created form for the Customers table is shown below.

Forms can be used to enter, change or view data. They are mainly used to improve the way in which data is displayed on the screen.

Forms can also be used to sort records in a database table in descending or ascending order of a selected field.

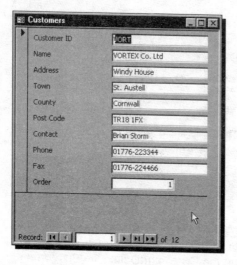

When you attempt to close a new **Form** window, you will be asked if you would like to save it. An Access database can have lots of different forms, each designed with a different purpose in mind. Saved forms are displayed in the Database window when you click the Forms button in the Objects menu. In the above example, we chose the default name suggested by Access, which was Customers.

In the next chapter we will discuss Form design in some detail, including their customisation.

Working with Data

Adding Records in a Table: Whether you are in Table view or Form view, to add a record, click the New Record icon, shown here.

When in Table view, the cursor jumps to the first empty record in the table (the one with the asterisk in the box to the left of the first field). When in Form view, Access displays an empty form which can be used to add a new record.

Finding Records in a Table: Whether you are in Table or Form view, to find a record click the Find icon, or use **Edit, Find**. This opens the following dialogue box:

Note the field name in the **Look In** box of the dialogue box, which is CustomerID, indicating that we are only interested in finding a match within the CustomerID field.

To find all the records starting with w, we type **w*** in the **Find What** box of the dialogue box. Pressing the **Find First** button, highlights the first record with the CustomerID 'WEST'. Pressing the **Find Next** button, highlights the next record that matches our selected criteria, which in this case will be 'WORM'.

Deleting Records from a Table: To delete a record when in Table view, point to the box to the left of the record to highlight the entire record, as shown below, then press the <Del> key.

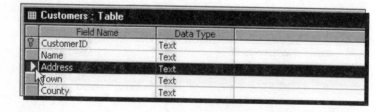

To delete a record when in Form view, first display the record you want to delete, then use the **Edit, Select Record** command to select the whole record, and press the <Del> key.

In both cases you will be given a warning and you will be asked to confirm your decision.

Delete, Insert, and Move Fields in a Table: To delete a field from a table, close any forms that might be open, then load the table from the Database window, then press the Design View button, click the row selector to highlight the field you want to remove, as shown below, and press the Delete Rows button, shown here, or use the **Edit, Delete** command.

▦ Customers : Table		
Field Name	Data Type	
⚷ CustomerID	Text	
Name	Text	
▶ Address	Text	
Town	Text	
County	Text	

To insert a field in a table, display the table in Design View, and highlight the field above which you want to insert the new field, and press the Insert Rows button, shown here, or use the **Insert, Rows** command.

To move a field from its current to a new position in a table, select the field you want to move in Design View, then point to the row selector so that the mouse pointer is inclined as shown below, and drag the row to its new position.

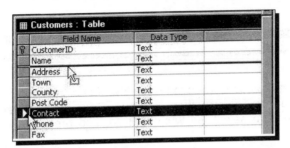

Note that while you are dragging the field, the mouse pointer changes to the one pointing at the Name field in the above composite. Releasing the mouse button, moves the Contact field to the position of the thin horizontal line and pushes all other fields below it one row down.

Printing a Table View

You can print a database table by clicking the Print icon, or

by using the **File, Print** command which displays the Print dialogue box shown below. Alternatively, you can preview a database on screen by clicking the Preview icon.

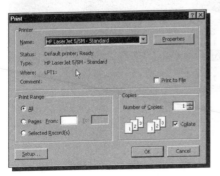

However, printing directly from here, produces a predefined printout, the format of which you cannot control, apart from the margins and print orientation. To control these, click the **Setup** or **Properties** button.

For a better method of producing a printed output, see the Report Design section in the next chapter.

Relational Database Design

In order to be able to discuss relational databases, we will add an Orders table to our database. To do this, carry out the following steps.

- Open the **Adept 1** database and with the Tables Object active, click the **New** Toolbar button.

- Use the Table Wizard and select Orders from the displayed **Sample Tables** list. Next, select the five fields displayed below under **Fields in my new table** from the **Sample Fields** list, and press **Next**.

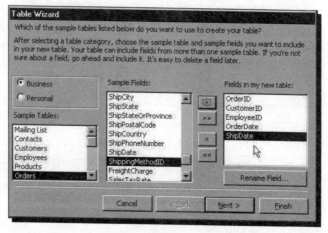

In the next four dialogue boxes, do the following:

- Accept the default name (Orders), click the **No, I'll set the primary key** radio button, and press **Next**.

- Accept the default field (OrderID) as the field which holds data that is unique to each record, click the **Numbers and/or letters I enter when I add new records** radio button and press **Next**.

- On the next dialogue box you specify whether the new table is related to any other tables in the database. Accept the default which is, that it is not related, and press **Next**.

Although the two tables are actually related, we chose at this stage to tell the Wizard that they are not. This might appear to you as odd, but the Wizard makes certain assumptions about unique fields (for example, that ID fields are numbers), which is not what we want them to be. We choose to remain in control of the design of our database and, therefore, we will define the relationship between the two tables later.

- In the final dialogue box, click the **Enter data directly into the table** radio button, and press **Finish**.

The Wizard displays the newly created table ready for you to enter your data. However, before doing so, use the Design Table facility, as discussed previously, to change the Data Types of the selected Field Names to those displayed here.

Orders : Table	
Field Name	Data Type
OrderID	Text
CustomerID	Text
EmployeeID	Text
OrderDate	Date/Time
ShipDate	Date/Time

The information you need to enter in the Orders table is shown below.

Order ID	Customer II	Employee ID	Order Date	Ship Date
99085VOR	VORT	A.D. Smith	20/03/99	10/04/99
99097AVO	AVON	W.A. Brown	25/03/99	14/04/99
99099BAR	BARR	S.F. Adams	01/04/99	02/05/99
99002STO	STON	C.H. Wills	20/04/99	25/05/99
99006PAR	PARK	A.D. Smith	13/05/99	16/06/99
99010WES	WEST	W.A. Brown	15/05/99	26/06/99
99018GLO	GLOW	L.S. Stevens	25/06/99	19/07/99
99025SIL	SILV	S.F. Adams	28/06/99	22/07/99
99029WOR	WORM	C.H. Wills	20/07/99	13/08/99
99039EAL	EALI	A.D. Smith	30/07/99	25/08/99
99045HIR	HIRE	W.A. Brown	18/08/99	08/09/99
99051EUR	EURO	L.S. Stevens	25/08/99	19/09/99
99064AVO	AVON	S.F. Adams	20/09/99	15/10/99

Record: 1 of 13

Relationships

Information held in two or more tables of a database is normally related in some way. In our case, the two tables, Customers and Orders, are related by the CustomerID field.

To build up relationships between tables, return to the Database window and press the Relationships icon on the Tool bar, shown here. This opens the following window in which the index field in each table is emboldened.

You can build relationships between tables by dragging a field name from one table into another. In our example below, we have dragged CustomerID from the Customers table (by pointing to it, pressing the left mouse button, and while keeping the mouse button pressed, dragging the pointer) to the required field in the other table, in this case CustomerID in the Orders table.

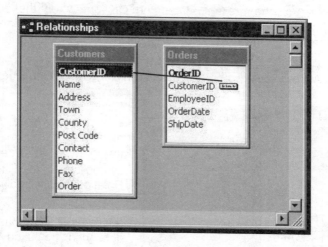

Releasing the mouse button opens the dialogue boxes shown at the top of the next page (the second one by pressing the **Join Type** button on the first one).

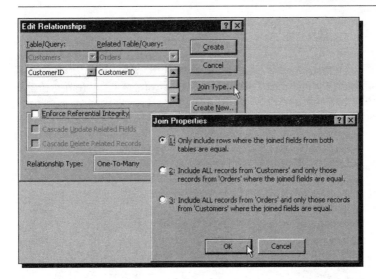

In the Join Properties dialogue box you can specify the type of join Access should create in new queries - more about this later. For the present, press the **OK** button on the Join Properties dialogue box, to close it, then check the **Enforce Referential Integrity** box in the Relationships dialogue box, and press the **Create** button.

Access creates and displays graphically the chosen type of

relationship in the Relationships window shown here. Note the relationship '1 customer to many (∞) orders' symbolism in the Relationships window.

Because Access is a relational database, data can be used in queries from more than one table at a time. As we have seen, if the database contains tables with related data, the relationships can be defined easily.

Usually, the matching fields have the same name, as in our example of Customers and Orders tables. In the Customers table, the CustomerID field is the primary field and relates to the CustomerID field in the Orders table - there can be several orders in the Orders table from one customer in the Customers table.

The various types of relationships are as follows:

- Inherited - for attaching tables from another Access database. The original relationships of the attached database can be used in the current database.

- Referential - for enforcing relationships between records according to certain rules, when you add or delete records in related tables within the same database. For example, you can only add records to a related table, if a matching record already exists in the primary table, and you cannot delete a record from the primary table if matching records exist in a related table.

Viewing and Editing Relationships

To view the current relationships between tables, activate the Database window and press the Relationships icon. This displays the following:

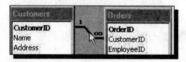

To edit a relationship, double-click the left mouse button at the pointer position shown here. The tip of the mouse pointer must be on the inclined line joining the two tables in the Relationships window, as shown, before Access will respond. If you have difficulty with this action, first point to the relationship line and click once to embolden it, then use the **Relationships, Edit Relationship** command. Either of these two actions will open the Relationships dialogue box in which you can change the various options already discussed.

To remove a relationship, activate it (point and click to embolden it), then press the <Del> key. To delete a table, you must first detach it from other tables, then select it in the Database Window and press the <Del> key.

Creating an Additional Table

As an exercise, create a third table using the Table Wizard and select Invoices from the displayed **Sample Tables** list. Then choose the five fields displayed below - the names and their data types have been changed using the Design Table facility.

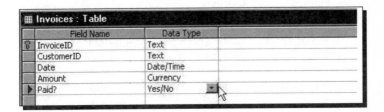

Field Name	Data Type
InvoiceID	Text
CustomerID	Text
Date	Date/Time
Amount	Currency
Paid?	Yes/No

Next, enter the data given below and build up appropriate relationships between the Invoices table, the Customers table and the Orders table, as shown on the next page.

Invoice No	Customer ID	Date	Amount	Paid?
AD9901	VORT	10/04/99	£120.84	No
AD9902	AVON	14/04/99	£103.52	Yes
AD9903	BARR	02/05/99	£99.32	No
AD9904	STON	25/05/99	£55.98	No
AD9905	PARK	16/06/99	£180.22	No
AD9906	WEST	26/06/99	£68.52	No
AD9907	GLOW	19/07/99	£111.56	No
AD9908	SILV	22/07/99	£123.45	Yes
AD9909	WORM	13/08/99	£35.87	No
AD9910	EALI	25/08/99	£58.95	No
AD9911	HIRE	08/09/99	£290.00	No
AD9912	EURO	19/09/99	£150.00	No
AD9913	AVON	15/10/99	£135.00	No
				No

The relationships between the three tables should be arranged as follows:

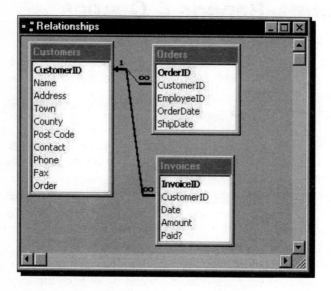

It is important that you should complete this exercise, as it consolidates what we have done so far and, in any case, we will be using all three tables in what comes next. So go ahead and try it.

13

Forms, Reports & Queries

In this chapter, we introduce the subject of Forms, Reports, and Queries. We will show you how to use the various Wizards to create:

- Forms to find, edit, and add data in a convenient manner. Access provides you with an easy way of designing various types of forms, some of which are discussed here. Forms look good on screen, but do not produce very good output on paper.

- Reports to produce good looking output on paper. However, reports do not necessarily look good on screen.

- Queries so that you can ask questions about the data in your database tables. For example, we could find out whether we have more than one order from the same customer in our Adept database.

Creating Forms

We saw in the previous chapter how easy it was to create a single column form to view our Customers table. To see this again, open **Adept 1** and in the Database window click the Forms button in the **Objects** list, as shown below, then double-click the entry Customers.

Using the Form Wizard

You can use the Form Wizard to easily display data from either a table or a query in form view.

In the Database window, first click the Forms button in the

Objects list, then the **New** button on the Toolbar, which opens the New Form dialogue box, shown below. As you can see from this screen dump, there are different types of forms available for you to choose from. Their function will be discussed shortly.

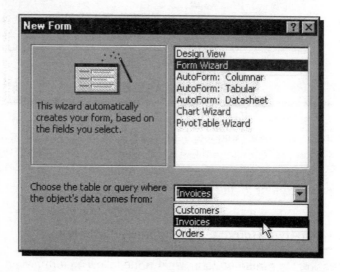

To continue with our example, we first selected the Form Wizard, then chose the Invoices table on which to base the new form, and pressed the **OK** button (which is obscured in the above screen dump by the drop-down list of database tables). This causes the Wizard to display the first of four additional dialogue boxes, shown on the next page, in which you are asked to specify the fields that contain the data you want to chart. We chose all the fields.

As usual, after making appropriate selections, click the **Next** button to progress through the automatic design of the particular form.

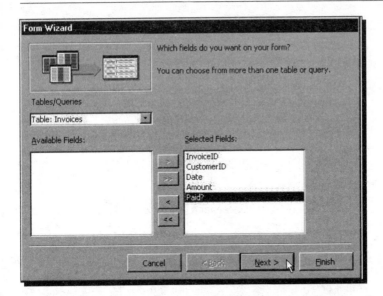

In the next three dialogue boxes that are displayed by the Wizard, make the following selections in order of appearance:

- **Columnar** for the layout of your form.

- **Standard** as the style for your Labels and Data.

- **Open the form to view or enter information**.

Pressing the **Finish** button, displays the following form.

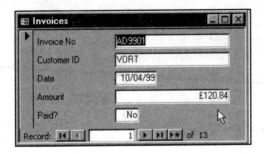

Types of Forms

The available choice of Form designs have the following function:

Type of Form	Function
Design View	Design a form from scratch.
Form Wizard	Automatically creates a form based on the fields you select.
AutoForm: Columnar	Creates a columnar form with all the field labels appearing in the first column and the data in the second. The form displays one record at a time.
AutoForm: Tabular	Tabulates a screen full of records in tabular form with the field labels appearing at the head of each column.
AutoForm: Datasheet	Similar to the Tabular form, but in worksheet display format.
Chart Wizard	Displays data graphically.
PivotTable Wizard	Creates a form with an Excel PivotTable - an interactive table that can summarise a large number of data using the format and calculation methods specified by the user.

Access also allows you to design a form that contains another form. This type of form, called main/subform, allows data from related tables to be viewed at the same time.

Subforms are especially effective when you want to show data from tables or queries with a one-to-many relationship. For example, you could create a form with a subform to show data from a Customers table and a Invoices table. The data in the Customers table is the 'one' side of the relationship, while the data in the invoices table is the 'many' side of the relationship - each customer can be issued with more than one invoice.

Customising a Form

You can customise a form by changing the appearance of
text, data, and any other attributes. To have a look

at some of these options, double-click on
Customers to display the Customers form, then
click the Design View button on the Toolbar.

What appears on your screen is shown below:

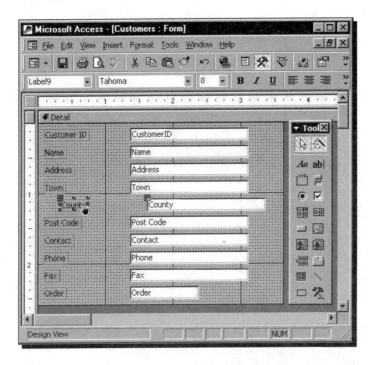

As you can see, a form in Design View is made up of boxes
attached to a grid. Clicking at the County box, for example,
causes markers to appear around it as shown above. When
the mouse pointer is then placed within either the label box or
data box, it changes to a hand (as shown), which indicates
that you can drag the box to a new position, as we have done
above. This method moves both label and data boxes
together.

If you look more closely at the markers around the label and data boxes, you will see that they are of different size, as shown below.

The larger ones are 'move' handles, while the smaller ones are 'size' handles. In the above example you can use the 'move' handles on either the label or the data box (as shown) to move one independently of the other. Note the shape of the hand in this case which is different to our previous screen dump.

The label box can also be sized. To size the data box, click on it so that the markers appear around it. Boxes on a form can be made larger by simply pointing to the sizing handles and dragging them in the appropriate direction.

In addition to moving and enlarging label and data boxes, you can further customise a form using the various new buttons that appear on the Tool bar when in Design View, shown below in two tiers.

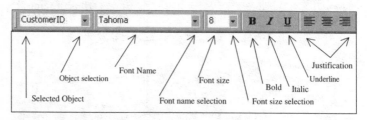

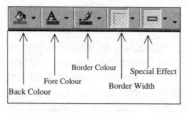

Do try and experiment with moving and sizing label and data boxes and also increasing their font size. If you don't like the result, simply don't save it. Skills gained here will be used in the Report design section.

The Toolbox

The Toolbox can be used either to design a Form or Report from scratch (a task beyond the scope of this book), or to add controls to them, such as a Combo (drop-down) box. The function of each tool on the Toolbox is listed below.

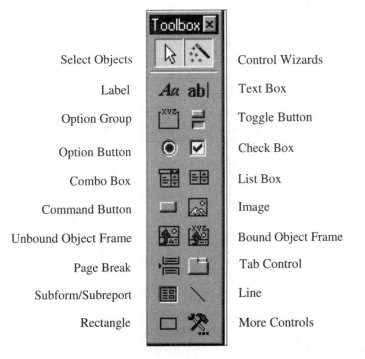

Select Objects	Control Wizards
Label	Text Box
Option Group	Toggle Button
Option Button	Check Box
Combo Box	List Box
Command Button	Image
Unbound Object Frame	Bound Object Frame
Page Break	Tab Control
Subform/Subreport	Line
Rectangle	More Controls

As an example of using the Toolbox, let us assume that we would like to use a form to enter new data into our Invoices table, but with the ability of selecting the CustomerID field from a drop-down menu - a Combo box.

To achieve the above, execute the following steps:

- On the Database window first click the Forms button in the **Objects** list, then double-click on Invoices. If you have not created the Invoice form, you must do so as explained in the 'Using the Form Wizard' section at the beginning of this chapter, before going on.

- When the Invoice form appears on the screen, click the Design View button on the Toolbar, and enlarge the Invoices form so that both the Header and Footer sections are visible on the form, as shown below.

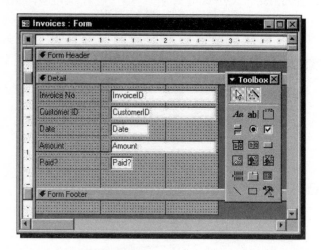

- Click the CustomerID field on the form, and delete both its Label and Data boxes by clicking each individually and pressing the <Del> key.

- Click the Combo Box on the Toolbox, and point and click at the area where the CustomerID field used to be on the form.

- In the subsequent dialogue boxes, select options which will cause the Combo Box to look up the values from the Customers table, and from the CustomerID field and store a selected value in the CustomerID field.

Specify that the Combo Box should have the label Customer ID:.

- Move and size both the Label and Data boxes of the Combo box into the position shown below.

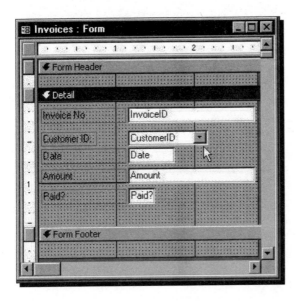

- Click the Form View button on the Toolbar, followed by the New Record button at the bottom of the Invoices form, both of which are shown below.

The entry form should now look as shown on the next page.

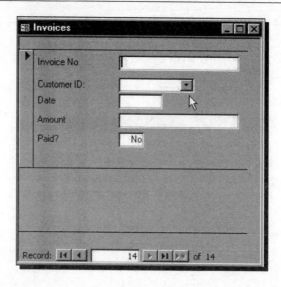

From now on, whenever you want to add a new invoice to the Invoices table, use the Invoices form from the Database window, then click the New Record button on either the Toolbar or the Invoices form itself to display an empty form.

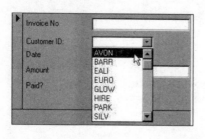

Next, type in the relevant information in the appropriate data boxes on the form, but when you come to fill in the Customer ID field, click instead the down arrow against its data box to display the drop-down menu shown here. Select one of the existing customers on the list, and click the Next Record button ▶ at the bottom of the Invoices form.

Try the above procedure with the following details:

```
AD9914      WEST      28/10/99      £140
```

then verify that indeed the information has been recorded by double-clicking the Invoices table on the Database window. Don't forget to save the changes to the Invoices form.

Using the Report Wizard

We will use the skills gained in manipulating Forms in Design View to produce an acceptable report created by the Report Wizard. To produce a report of the Invoices table, do the following:

- Click the Reports button in the **Objects** list on the Database window and then press the **New** button.

- In the New Report dialogue box, select the **Report Wizard** option, and choose 'Invoices' as the table where the object's data will come from, and press **OK**.

- Select all the fields (except for the Paid? field) which are to appear on your report and click the **Next** button.

- Select the InvoiceID field as the sort field, and accept all subsequent default settings. Call the report 'Invoices'. The report is created for you, the top portion of which is shown below.

Invoices

CustomerID	Invoice No	Date	Amount
AVON			
	AD 9902	14/04/99	£103.52
	AD 9913	15/10/99	£135.00
BARR			
	AD 9903	02/05/99	£99.32
EALI			
	AD 9910	25/08/99	£58.95
EURO			
	AD 9912	19/09/99	£150.00
GLOW			
	AD 9907	19/07/99	£111.56
HIRE			
	AD 9911	08/09/99	£290.00
PARK			
	AD 9905	16/06/99	£180.22
SILV			
	AD 9908	22/07/99	£123.45

Creating a Query

You create a query so that you can ask questions about the data in your database tables. For example, we could find out whether we have more than one order from the same customer in our Adept database.

To do this, start Access, open **Adept 1**, and in the Database window click the Queries button in the **Objects** list, followed by the **New** button which opens the New Query dialogue box. Selecting the **Find Duplicates Query Wizard**, displays the following:

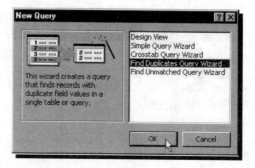

On clicking **OK**, the Find Duplicates Query Wizard dialogue box is displayed, as shown below, in which choose the orders table. Next, select the Orders table from the displayed database tables in this dialogue box, and press the **Next** button.

On the following dialogue box select **CustomerID** as the field you want to check for duplicate values, then press the 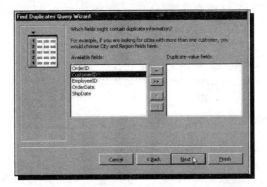 button, followed by the **Next** button.

Finally, select the additional fields you would like to see along with the duplicate values, by selecting those you want from the next dialogue box, either one at a time or, if you decide to select all of them, as shown here, by clicking the 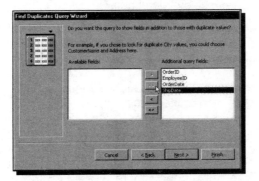 button.

Clicking the **Finish** button displays the Select Query screen shown below.

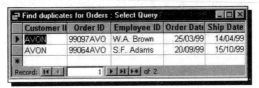

Types of Queries

The query we have created so far, is known as the *Select Query*, which is the most common type of query. However, with Access you can also create and use other types of queries, as follows:

- **Crosstab query** - used to present data with row and column headings, just like a spreadsheet. It can be used to summarise large amounts of data in a more readable form.

- **Action query** - used to make changes to many records in one operation. For example, you might like to remove from a given table all records that meet certain criteria, make a new table, or append records to a table. Obviously, this type of query has to be treated with care!

- **Union query** - used to match fields from two or more tables.

- **Pass-through query** - used to pass commands to a SQL (see below) database.

- **Data-definition query** - used to create, change, or delete tables in an Access database using SQL statements.

SQL stands for Structured Query Language, often used to query, update, and manage relational databases. Each query created by Access has an associated SQL statement that defines the action of that query. Thus, if you are familiar with SQL, you can use such statements to view and modify queries, or set form and report properties. However, these actions can be done more easily with the QBE (query-by-example) grid, to be discussed next. If you design union queries, pass-through queries, or data-definition queries, then you must use SQL statements, as these types of queries can not be designed with the QBE grid. Finally, to create a sub-query, you use the QBE grid, but you enter a SQL SELECT statement for criteria, as we shall see in the next QBE grid example.

The Query Window

The Query window is a graphical query-by-example (QBE) tool. Because of Access' graphical features, you can use the mouse to select, drag, and manipulate objects in the query window to define how you would like to see your data.

An example of a ready made Query window can be seen by selecting the Find duplicates for Orders query and clicking the **Design** button on the Database window. This action opens the Select Query dialogue box shown below.

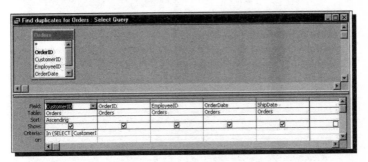

You can add a table to the top half of the Query window by dragging the table from the Database window. Similarly, you can add fields to the bottom half of the Query window (the QBE grid) by dragging fields from the tables on the top half of the Query window. In addition, the QBE grid is used to select the sort order of the data, or insert criteria, such as SQL statements.

To see the full SQL SELECT statement written by Access as the criteria selection when we first defined the query, use the **View, SQL View** command.

Note the part of the statement which states 'As Tmp GROUP'. Access collects the data you want as a temporary group, called a *dynaset*. This special set of data behaves like a table, but is not a table; it is a dynamic view of the data from one or more tables, selected and sorted by the particular query.

Adding Tables to a Query Window

Below, we show a screen dump created by first clicking the Queries button in the **Objects** list, then pressing the **New** button on the Database window. In the displayed New Query dialogue box, select Design View, as shown below, and press the **OK** button.

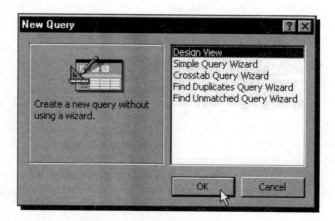

This opens both the Select Query and the Show Table dialogue boxes shown below. The Invoices and Customers tables were then added to the Select Query window by selecting then in the Show Table dialogue box and pressing the **Add** button, as shown below.

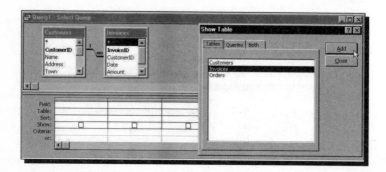

Adding Fields to a Query Window

Below we show a screen in which the Paid?, InvoiceID, and Amount fields have been dragged from the Invoices table and added to the Query window. Also, the Name and Contact fields have been dragged from the Customers table and placed on the Query window, while the Phone field from the Customers table is about to be added to the Query window.

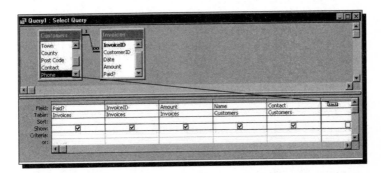

Having dragged all five fields from the two tables onto the QBE grid, we have added the word No as the criteria on the Paid? field and selected Ascending as the Sort for the InvoiceID field.

Note that the Invoices and Customers tables are joined by a line that connects the two CustomerID fields. The join line was created when we designed the tables and their relationships in the previous chapter. Even if you have not created these relationships, Access will join the tables in a query automatically when the tables are added to a query, provided each table has a field with the same name and a compatible data type and one of those fields is a primary key. A primary field is displayed in bold in the Query window.

If you have not created relationships between your tables yourself, or Access has not joined your tables automatically, you can still use related data in your query by joining the tables in the Query window.

Clicking the Run icon on the Toolbar, shown here, instantly displays all the unpaid invoices with the details you have asked for, as follows:

Paid?	Invoice No	Amount	Name	Contact	Phone
No	AD9901	£120.84	VORTEX Co. Ltd	Brian Storm	01776-223344
No	AD9903	£99.32	BARROWS Associates	Mandy Brown	01554-664422
No	AD9904	£55.98	STONEAGE Ltd	Mike Irons	01765-234567
No	AD9905	£180.22	PARKWAY Gravel	James Stone	01534-987654
No	AD9906	£68.52	WESTWOOD Ltd	Mary Slim	01234-667755
No	AD9907	£111.56	GLOWORM Ltd	Peter Summers	01432-746523
No	AD9909	£35.87	WORMGLAZE Ltd	Richard Glazer	01123-654321
No	AD9910	£58.95	EALING Engines Design	Trevor Miles	01336-010107
No	AD9911	£290.00	HIRE Service Equipment	Nicole Webb	01875-558822
No	AD9912	£150.00	EUROBASE Co. Ltd	Sarah Star	01736-098765
No	AD9913	£135.00	AVON Construction	John Waters	01657-113355
No	AD9914	£140.00	WESTWOOD Ltd	Mary Slim	01234-667755

Record: 1 of 12

To save your newly created query, use the **File, Save As** command, and give it a name such as 'Unpaid Invoices' in the Save As dialogue box.

Types of Criteria

Access accepts the following expressions as criteria:

Arithmetic Operators		Comparison Operators		Logical Operators	
*	Multiply	<	Less than	And	And
/	Divide	<=	Less than or equal	Or	Inclusive or
+	Add	>	Greater than	Xor	Exclusive or
-	Subtract	>=	Greater than or equal	Not	Not equivalent
		=	Equal	Eqv	Equivalent
		<>	Not equal	Imp	Implication

Other operators		
Between	Between 50 And 150	All values between 50 and 150
In	In("Bath","Bristol")	All records with Bath and Bristol
Is	Is Null	All records with no value in that field
Like	Like "Brian *"	All records with Brian something in field
&	[Name]&" "&[Surname]	Concatenates strings

Using Wildcard Characters in Criteria

In the previous example we used the criteria A* to mean any company whose name starts with the letter A. The asterisk in this criteria is known as a wildcard character.

To search for a pattern, you can use the asterisk (*) and the question mark (?) as wildcard characters when specifying criteria in expressions. An asterisk stands for any number of characters, while a question mark stands for any single character in the same position as the question mark.

The following examples show the use of wildcard characters in various types of expressions:

Entered Expression	Meaning	Examples
a?	Any two-letter word beginning with A	am, an, as, at
???d	Any four-letter word ending with d	find, hand, land yard
Sm?th	Any five-letter word beginning with Sm and ending with th	Smith Smyth
fie*	Any word starting with the letters fie	field, fiend, fierce, fiery
*ght	Any word ending with ght	alight, eight, fight, light, might, sight
*/5/97	All dates in May '97	1/5/97
a	Any word with the letter a in it	Brian, Mary, star, yard

Combining Criteria

By specifying additional criteria in a Query window you can create powerful queries for viewing your data. In the examples below we have added the field Amount to our Unpaid Invoices query.

The AND Criteria with Different Fields: When you insert criteria in several fields, but in the same row, Access assumes that you are searching for records that meet all of the criteria. For example, the criteria below lists the records shown.

The OR Criteria with the Same Field: If you include multiple criteria in one field only, then Access assumes that you are searching for records that meet any one of the specified criteria. For example, the criteria <50 or >100 in the field Amount, shown below, list the required records, only if the No in the Paid? field is inserted in both rows.

The OR Criteria with Different Fields: If you include multiple criteria in different fields, but in different rows, then Access assumes that you are searching for records that meet either one or the other of the specified criteria. For example, the criteria Yes in the Paid? field and the criteria <50 in the Amount field, but in different rows, list the following records.

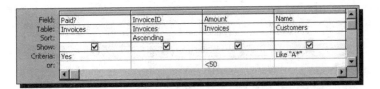

Field:	Paid?	InvoiceID	Amount	Name
Table:	Invoices	Invoices	Invoices	Customers
Sort:		Ascending		
Show:	☑	☑	☑	☑
Criteria:	Yes			
or:			<50	

Query1 : Select Query

	Paid?	Invoice No	Amount	Name	Contact	Phone
▶	Yes	AD9902	£103.52	AVON Construction	John Waters	01657-113355
	Yes	AD9908	£123.45	SILVERSMITH Co	Adam Smith	01336-997755
	No	AD9909	£35.87	WORMGLAZE Ltd	Richard Glazer	01123-654321

Record: 1 of 3

The AND and OR Criteria Together: The following choice of criteria will cause Access to retrieve either records that have Yes in the Paid? field and the company's name starts with the letter A, or records that the invoice amount is less than £50.

Field:	Paid?	InvoiceID	Amount	Name
Table:	Invoices	Invoices	Invoices	Customers
Sort:		Ascending		
Show:	☑	☑	☑	☑
Criteria:	Yes			Like "A*"
or:			<50	

Unpaid Invoices : Select Query

	Paid?	Invoice No	Amount	Name	Contact	Phone
▶	Yes	AD9902	£103.52	AVON Construction	John Waters	01657-113355
	No	AD9909	£35.87	WORMGLAZE Ltd	Richard Glazer	01123-654321

Record: 1 of 2

Calculating Totals in Queries

Access allows you to perform calculations on groups of records. For example, we could find the total value of unpaid invoices grouped by month. To do this, start a new query in Design View, and using the Invoices table, drag the 'Paid?' And 'Amount' fields into the Query window, as shown below. Then enter in the third column (Field row) the formula

```
Month:DatePart("m",(Date))
```

Functions, such as 'sum', are entered in the Total row of a query which can be displayed by clicking the Totals button, shown to the left, while in Design View. Save this query under the name 'Monthly Invoices', then click the **Run** button on the Toolbar to see the result.

Field:	Paid?	Amount	Month: DatePart("m",[Date])
Table:	Invoices	Invoices	
Total:	Group By	Sum	Group By
Sort:			
Show:	☑	☑	☑
Criteria:	No		
or:			

Monthly Invoices : Select Query

Paid?	SumOfAmount	Month
No	£120.84	4
No	£155.30	5
No	£248.74	6
No	£111.56	7
No	£94.82	8
No	£440.00	9
No	£275.00	10

Record: 1 of 7

* * *

We hope we have covered enough features of the program in this book to give you the foundations needed to make you want to explore Access more fully by yourself.

However, if you would prefer to be guided through these and additional topics, in much more detail, then may we suggest you look up the book *Microsoft Access 2000 explained* (BP474), also published by BERNARD BABANI (publishing) Ltd.

14

Sharing Information

You can link or embed all or part of an existing file created either in an Office application or in any other application that supports Object Linking and Embedding (OLE). However, if an application does not support OLE, then you must use the copy/cut and paste commands to copy or move information from one application to another. In general, you copy, move, link, embed, or hyperlink information depending on the imposed situation, as follows:

Imposed Situation	Method to Adopt
Inserted information will not need updating, or Application does not support OLE.	Copy or move
Inserted information needs to be automatically updated in the destination file as changes are made to the data in the source file, or Source file will always be available and you want to minimise the size of the destination file, or Source file is to be shared amongst several users.	Link
Inserted information might need to be updated but source file might not be always accessible, or Destination files needs to be edited without having these changes reflected in the source file.	Embed
To jump to a location in a document or Web page, or to a file that was created in a different program.	Hyperlink

Copying or Moving Information

To copy or move information between programs running under Windows, such as Microsoft applications, is extremely easy. To move information, use the drag and drop facility, while to copy information, use the **Edit, Copy** and **Edit, Paste** commands.

To illustrate the technique, we will copy the **Project 3.xls** file, created in Excel, into Word. We will consider the following two possibilities:

Source File Available without Application

Let us assume that you only have the source file **Project 3.xls** on disc, but not the application that created it (that is you don't have Excel). In such a situation, you can only copy the contents of the whole file to the destination (in our case Word). To achieve this, do the following:

- Start Word and minimise it on the Taskbar.

- Use My Computer (or Explorer) to locate the file whose contents you want to copy into Word.

- Click the filename that you want to copy, hold the mouse button down and point to Word on the Taskbar until the application opens.

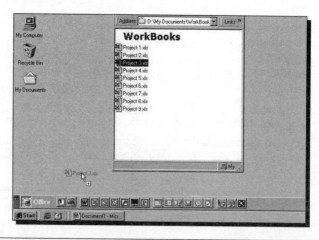

- While still holding the mouse button down, move the mouse pointer into Word's open document to the exact point where you would like to insert the contents of **Project 3.xls**.

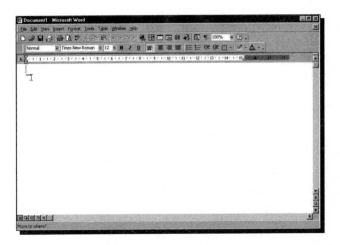

- Release the mouse button to place the contents of **Project 3.xls** into Word at that point.

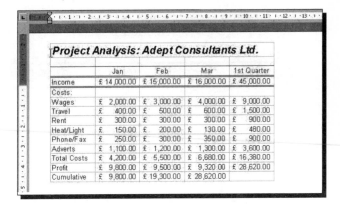

Project Analysis: Adept Consultants Ltd.

	Jan	Feb	Mar	1st Quarter
Income	£ 14,000.00	£ 15,000.00	£ 16,000.00	£ 45,000.00
Costs:				
Wages	£ 2,000.00	£ 3,000.00	£ 4,000.00	£ 9,000.00
Travel	£ 400.00	£ 500.00	£ 600.00	£ 1,500.00
Rent	£ 300.00	£ 300.00	£ 300.00	£ 900.00
Heat/Light	£ 150.00	£ 200.00	£ 130.00	£ 480.00
Phone/Fax	£ 250.00	£ 300.00	£ 350.00	£ 900.00
Adverts	£ 1,100.00	£ 1,200.00	£ 1,300.00	£ 3,600.00
Total Costs	£ 4,200.00	£ 5,500.00	£ 6,680.00	£ 16,380.00
Profit	£ 9,800.00	£ 9,500.00	£ 9,320.00	£ 28,620.00
Cumulative	£ 9,800.00	£ 19,300.00	£ 28,620.00	

Source File and Application Available

Assuming that you have both the file and the application that created it on your computer, you can copy all or part of the contents of the source file to the destination file. To achieve this, do the following:

- Start Excel and open **Project 3.xls**.

- Highlight as much information as you would like to copy and click the copy icon on the Toolbar.

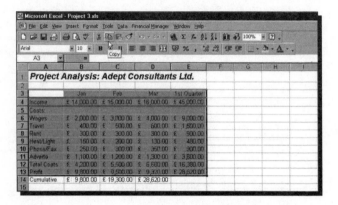

- Start Word and click the Paste icon on the Toolbar.

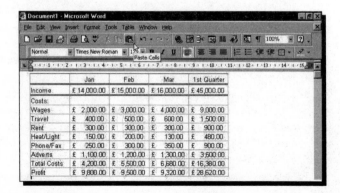

Object Linking and Embedding

Object Linking is copying information from one file (the source file) to another file (the destination file) and maintaining a connection between the two files. When information in the source file is changed, then the information in the destination file is automatically updated. Linked data is stored in the source file, while the file into which you place the data stores only the location of the source and displays a representation of the linked data.

For example, you would use Object Linking if you would want an Excel chart included in, say, a Word document to be updated whenever you changed the information used to create the chart in the first place within Excel. In such a case, the Excel worksheet containing the chart would be referred to as the source file, while the Word document would be referred to as the destination file.

Object Embedding is inserting information created in one file (the source file) into another file (the container file). After such information has been embedded, the object becomes part of the container file. When you double-click an embedded object, it opens in the application in which it was created in the first place. You can then edit it in place, and the original object in the source application remains unchanged.

Thus, the main differences between linking and embedding are where the data is stored and how it is updated after you place it in your file. Linking saves you disc space as only one copy of the linked object is kept on disc. Embedding a logo chosen for your headed paper, saves the logo with every saved letter!

In what follows, we will discuss how you can link or embed either an entire file or selected information from an existing file, and how you can edit an embedded object. Furthermore, we will examine how to mail merge a letter written in Word with a list created either in Access, Excel, Outlook, or even Word itself.

Embedding a New Object

To embed a new object into an application, do the following:

- Open the container file, say Word, and click where you want to embed the new object.

- Use the **Insert, Picture** command, to display the additional drop-down menu, shown below.

- From this last drop-down menu action **Clip Art**, click the category you want and select a graphic.

As an example, we selected **Clip Art** (you could select a different option) and chose the Animal category from which we selected the graphic shown here. Clicking the **Insert Clip** button on the drop-down menu, embeds the selected object within Word.

Right-clicking such an embedded object displays a drop-down menu and selecting the **Edit Picture** option, opens up the Draw application which we used to add the perch. Once an embedded picture has been edited, double-clicking on it opens up the application used to edit it in the first place (the Draw application in our case), otherwise it opens the Format Picture dialogue box. Do try it for yourself.

Linking or Embedding an Existing File

To embed an existing file in its entirety into another application, do the following:

- Open the container file, say Word, and click where you want to embed the file.

- Use the **Insert, Object** command, to open the Object dialogue box, shown below, when the **Create from File** tab is clicked.

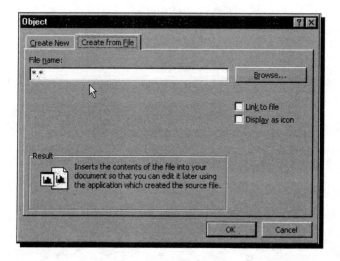

To locate the file you want to link or embed, click **Browse**, and then select the options you want.

- In the **File Name** box, type the name of the file you want to link or embed.

- To maintain a link to the original file, check the **Link to file** box.

Note: To insert graphics files, use the **Insert, Picture, From File** command instead of the **Insert, Object** command. This displays the Insert Picture dialogue box which allows you to specify within the **Look in** box the folder and file you want to insert.

Linking or Embedding Selected Information

To link or embed selected information from an existing file created in one application into another, do the following:

- Select the information in the source file you want to link or embed.

- Use the **Edit, Copy** command to copy the selected information to the Clipboard.

- Switch to the container file or document in which you want to place the information, and then click where you want the information to appear.

- Use the **Edit, Paste Special** command to open the following dialogue box:

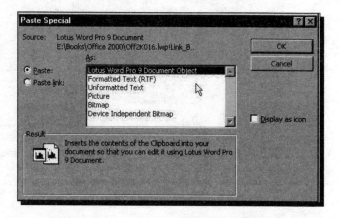

- To link the information, click the **Paste link** radio button, or to embed the information, click the **Paste** radio button. In the **As** box, click the item with the word 'Object' in its name. For example, if you copied the information from a Lotus Word Pro document, as we have for this example, the Word Pro Document Object appears in the **As** box. Select this object and press **OK**.

Linking or Embedding into Access

When you link or embed an object in a Microsoft Access form or report, the object is displayed in an object frame. To illustrate this point, start Access, select the Forms tab, and open Form1 (created in Chapter 12). Then do the following:

- Switch to Design View, then use the **Insert, Object** command, select the source application from the **Object Type** list in the Insert Object dialogue box (we chose the Microsoft Clip Gallery), and press **OK**.

- Select a graphic and click the **Insert Clip** button on the drop-down menu to insert it into an unbound frame which you might have to re-size. To force the graphic to fit into a smaller frame, right-click it, select **Properties** from the drop-down menu, click the down-arrow against the **Size Mode** box, and choose **Zoom**.

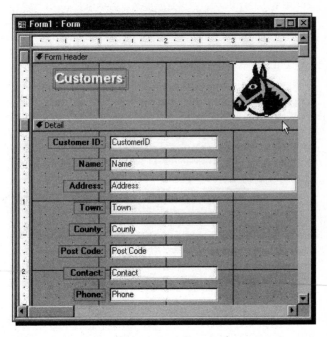

If the object you are embedding is from an Access table, use a bound object frame.

Editing an Embedded Object

If the application in which you created an embedded object is installed on your computer, double-click the object to open it for editing. Some applications start the original application in a separate window and then open the object for editing, while other applications temporarily replace the menus and toolbars in the current application so that you can edit the embedded object in place, without switching to another window.

To edit an embedded object which was inserted into a Microsoft Access form or report, first switch to Design View, then double-click the object to open the application on which it was created.

If the application in which an embedded object was created is not installed on your computer, convert the object to the file format of an application you do have. For example, if your Word document contains an embedded Microsoft Works Spreadsheet object and you do not have Works, you can convert the object to an Excel Workbook format and edit it in Excel.

Some embedded objects, such as sound and video clips, when double-clicked start playing their contents, instead of opening an application for editing. To illustrate this, copy either the **tutor.mpg** media file from its folder in the Windows 98 CD or the **goodtime.avi** video file from its folder in the Windows 95 CD, into Word using the **Copy, Paste Special** command (click the **Paste** radio button and the **Display as** **icon** box on the displayed dialogue box), and click **OK** to paste the required icon. The **tutor** file is to be found in the **cdsample, videos** folder, while the **goodtime** file is to be found in the **funstaff, videos, highperf** folder. The former places a Windows Media Player icon in your document, as shown here. Double-clicking such an icon, starts the video.

To edit one of these objects, select it and use the **Edit {Media Clip Object}, Edit** command. What appears within the curly brackets here, depends on the selected object; media clip in this case.

Hypertext Links

The main applications in Office 2000, Word, Access, and Excel, now support hyperlinks. A hyperlink causes a jump to another location in the current document or Web page, to a different Word document or Web page, or to a file that was created in a different program. You can, for example, jump from a Word document to an Excel worksheet or to a PowerPoint slide to see more detail.

A hyperlink is represented by a 'hot' image or by display text (which is often blue and underlined) that you click to jump to a different location. To insert a hyperlink into Word,

 Access, or Excel files and Web pages, select the display text or image, and either use the **Insert, Hyperlink** command or click the Insert Hyperlink button on the Standard Toolbar. Either action opens a dialogue box which allows you to browse for the destination address.

To illustrate the procedure, start Word, open the **PC Users4** memo, and highlight the word 'Explorer' to be found towards the end of it. Next, click the Hyperlink icon and locate the **explorer.exe** file (in the **Windows** folder) using the **Browse** button, as shown below.

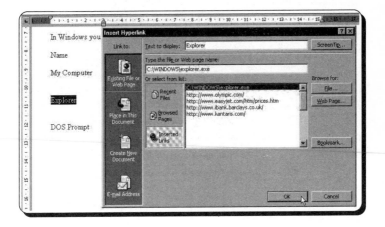

Pressing the **OK** button, underlines the highlighted text and changes its colour to blue. Pointing to such a hyperlink, changes the mouse pointer to a hand, as shown here, and left-clicking it, starts the Explorer. When you have finished using the Explorer, click its Close button for the program to return you automatically to the hyperlinked Word document.

If the location of the file you wanted to hyperlink to is incorrect, or you did not highlight the word to be used as the hyperlink, then errors will occur. If that is the case, place the insertion pointer within the hyperlink word, click the Insert Hyperlink icon again, and press the **Remove Link** button at the bottom left of the displayed Edit Hyperlink dialogue box.

As a second example, let us add to the **PC Users4** memo the following lines:

> Hyperlinks can be used for displaying additional information, such as an Excel sheet, or a PowerPoint slide.

and save the result as **PC Users5**. However, before you can use a range of cells in an Excel Workbook as your hyperlinked object, you must first name such a range. Therefore, start Excel, open the **Project 9** file and highlight the cell range A3:F13 in the Consolidation sheet, then use the **Insert, Name, Define** command and in the **Names in workbook** text box type Year_Summary (named ranges mustn't have spaces between words, hence the underscore). Next, save your changes to **Project 9** and exit Excel.

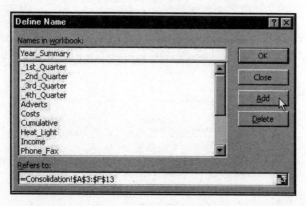

Finally, select the word 'sheet' in the Word document to use it as the hyperlink to **Project 9.xls** and browse to the location of the required file, then type after the filename the hash (#) character followed by the name of the required range, as shown below.

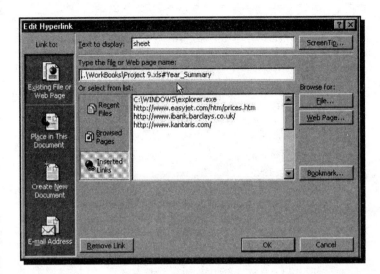

Left-clicking the hyperlink in Word will start Excel, open up the **Project 9** file, and display the named 'Year_Summary' range.

For the PowerPoint object, you could select the word 'slide' to use as the hyperlink to **Training 3.ppt**. If you wanted to make the link to a specific slide, then type # followed by the number of the required slide. Below we show the full address of such a hyperlink.

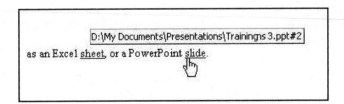

Mail Merging Lists

There are times when you may want to send the same basic letter to several different people, or companies. The easiest way to do this is with a Merge operation. Two files are prepared; a 'Data' file with the names and addresses, and a 'Form' file, containing the text and format of the letter. The two files are then merged together to produce a third file containing an individual letter to each party listed in the original data file.

Before creating a list of names and addresses for a mail merge, you need to select the Office application that is most suited to the task. For a mail merge, you can use a list you create in Access, Excel, Outlook, or Microsoft Word.

- For a long list in which you expect to add, change, or delete records, and for which you want a powerful sorting and searching capabilities to your disposal, you should use either Access or Excel, then specify the appropriate data file in the Word Mail Merge Helper (see below).

- To use the list of names and addresses in your Outlook Contact List, you select this list in the Word Mail Merge Helper.

- For a small to medium size list of names and addresses in which you do not expect to make many changes, you could elect to create a list in the Word Mail Merge Helper.

The Word Mail Merger Helper is a dialogue box in which you specify:

(a) whether you want to create form letters, labels, or print envelopes,

(b) where your list of names and addresses (data) is to be found, and

(c) what query options are to be applied to your data list before the merging process starts. These will be explained next with illustrated examples.

We will illustrate the merge procedure by using a memo created in Word (**PC Users1**) and a table which can be created in Word, or already exists either in an electronic book such as Outlook, in Excel or in an Access table such as Customers in **Adept 1**.

No matter which method you choose, first start Word and open the **PC Users1** memo (or your own letter), then provide two empty lines at the very top of the memo/letter by placing the insertion pointer at the beginning of the memo and pressing <Enter> twice. Then select these two empty lines and choose the Normal paragraph style.

Next, select **Tools, Mail Merge** which displays the Mail Merge Helper dialogue box shown below.

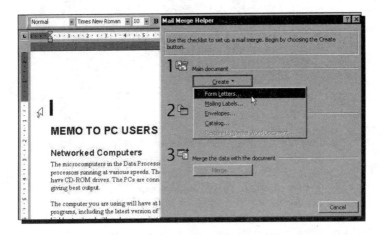

In this box, you define in three successive steps:

1. The document to be used,

2. The source of your data, and

3. The merging of the two.

Start by clicking the **Create** button, select the **Form Letters** option, and click the **Active Window** button.

Next, click the **Get Data** button which causes a drop-down menu to display, shown below.

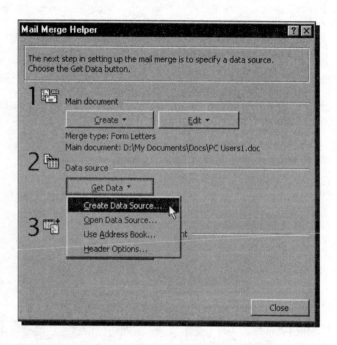

It is from this menu that you can select either to create your data source (the list of addresses) in Word, open (or import) an existing list of addresses which might be found in either Word, Excel, Access, etc., or use a list of contacts in an electronic address book such as Outlook.

In what follows, we will examine each of these options (in the same order as the list in the above drop-down menu). You can, of course, skip the Create an Address List in Word section, if you already have an existing data list.

Creating an Address List in Word

Selecting the **Create Data Source** menu option, displays the following dialogue box.

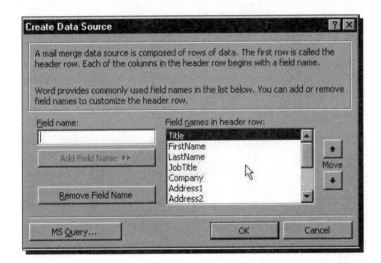

As you can see, Word provides commonly used field names for your address list. Unwanted field names can be deleted from the list by selecting them and pressing the **Remove Field Name** button. To add your own field name, type it in the **Field Name** box and press the **Add Field Name** button. The **Move** buttons to the right of the list can be used to move a selected field in the list to the top or bottom of the list by pressing the up-arrow or down-arrow, respectively.

Having compiled the required field names for your list, pressing the **OK** button, displays a Save As dialogue box, in which you can name your data list, say **Address**. Word automatically adds the file extension **.doc**, and displays the following warning dialogue box which allows you to either edit the data source or the main document.

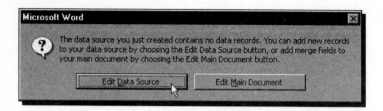

Press the **Edit Data Source** button if you want to create or edit your data list. Doing so displays the following Data Form dialogue box.

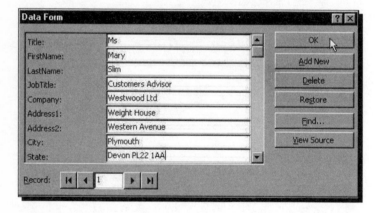

Here you can create a new data list or edit an existing one. We have typed in one fictitious entry in order to demonstrate the process, but we have not attempted to change the field names provided in any way whatsoever.

Having created a Word data list, added to one or edited one, pressing **OK** saves your changes to the already existing filename.

What follows is common to all existing data files, no matter in which application you chose to create it.

Getting an Address List

If you have not done so already, open the letter you want to mail merge, place the cursor in the position you want the address to appear, and select **Tools, Mail Merge** in Word. Then press the **Create** button in the Mail Merge Helper and choose **Form Letters, Active Window**.

Next, click the **Get Data** button (the 2nd step in the Mail

Merge Helper) which causes a drop-down menu, shown here, to display.

Select the **Open Data Source** option, and in the displayed dialogue box, select the drive, and click the down-arrow on the **Files of type** box. From here you can

choose the type of file that holds your address list, which could be one created in Word or a text editor (or exported in that form from another application), or an Access or Excel file.

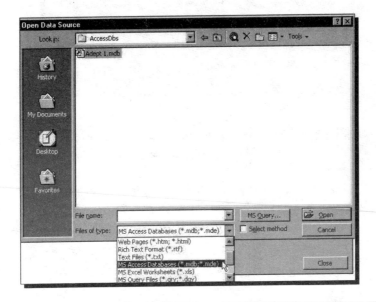

For our example we chose the **MS Access Database** type of file, which lists the databases on the specified drive and path. Next, select the database that holds your address data (in this case **Adept 1.mdb**) and click the **Open** button. Access is then loaded and the tables within the selected database are listed, as shown below.

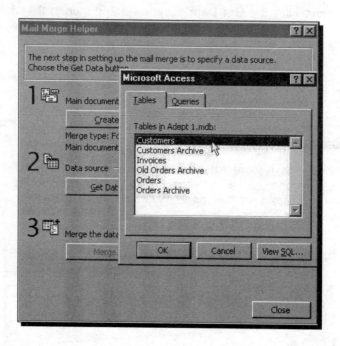

Microsoft Access then asks you to choose the Table that contains your data. In this case, select Customers and click the **OK** button.

Microsoft Word now displays a warning message, shown overleaf, to the effect that no merge fields have been found on your document.

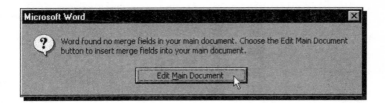

Don't worry about this, as we will rectify this omission, as follows:

- Click the **Edit Main Document** button on the above warning box which displays your document with an additional toolbar below the Formatting bar, as follows:

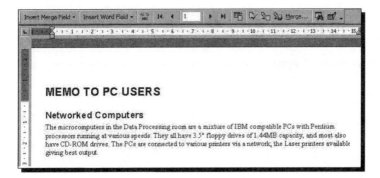

- Click the **Insert Merge Field** button on the new toolbar. This displays the fields in your Customers table.

- Select in turn, Name, Address, Town, County, and Post_Code. The first three are placed on the document on separate lines (by pressing <Enter> after each selection), while the last two are placed on the same line, but separated by a space. Finally, type on a new line the letters FAO: plus a space, and place the Contact field against it.

The first few lines of your document should now look as follows:

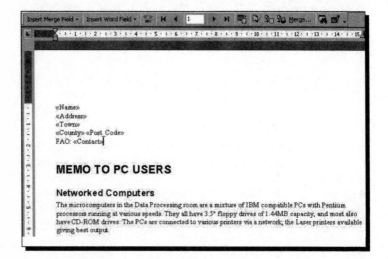

- Click the View Merged Data icon, shown to the right, to see your merged data. Clicking this icon once more, returns you to the screen above so that you can edit your work, or add merge fields.

- Click either the Merge to New Document icon or the Merge to Printer icon to create a new merged document to file or send the merged document to the printer.

That's all there is to it. You will possibly find it takes as little time to do, as it did to read about it!

15

Microsoft Publisher 2000

Microsoft Publisher is a desktop publishing program that allows you to quickly and easily create great-looking results that you can print on either your own printer, a commercial printer, or publish on the World Wide Web.

You can use Publisher to either design a publication from scratch with a variety of blank page templates whose margins and folds are already laid out for you, or use one of several Wizards that help you add your own contents to professionally designed templates under different categories. There are Wizards that you can use to create common types of publications, such as Newsletters, Brochures, Postcards, Signs, and Web sites, to mention but a few, with each type of publication offering different designs that you can choose from.

Whichever method you use, the program provides you with ease of use, and advanced desktop publishing features, including the ability to select a variety of colour schemes. In addition, you can put to use all the skills gained in Microsoft Word to create professional looking output.

Starting Publisher

Publisher is started in Windows either by clicking the **Start** button then selecting **Programs** and clicking on the

'Microsoft Publisher' icon on the cascade menu, clicking the Publisher button or the 'Open Office Document' icon on the Office Shortcut Bar, or by clicking and double-clicking on a Publisher file. In the latter case the document will be loaded into Publisher at the same time.

When you start Publisher by either of the first two methods, the 'Microsoft Publisher Catalog' box is displayed in the middle of your screen, as shown below.

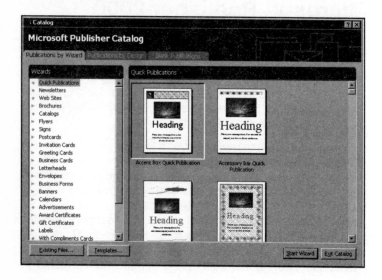

Note the three tabs at the top of the screen; the first two employ Wizards, while the last one lets you design your publication from scratch. Also note that a small triangle against a Wizard category indicates the existence of sub-categories, each one of which contains a variety of additional designs.

Once you have chosen a design and pressed the **Start Wizard** button, the following information box is displayed:

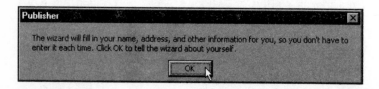

Pressing the **OK** button displays the dialogue box shown on the next page.

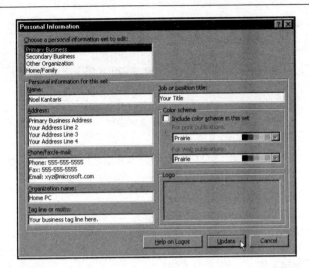

Publisher is asking you to enter personal details, so they can be used to fill in certain types of publications, such as business cards, automatically. Having filled in this dialogue box, press the **Update** button to start the design process.

Creating a Publication Using a Wizard

Below we follow step-by-step what would happen had you selected, say, the Arcs Quick Publication Wizard.

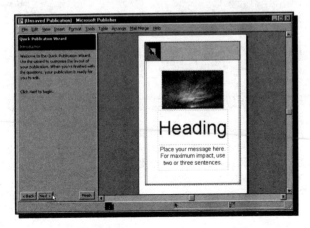

In the next three dialogue boxes, the Wizard asks you to select the following:

- The colour scheme of the page (not the graphic) - we chose 'Aqua'.

- The position of the graphic on the page, and where the message, if any, should appear - we chose to leave these as they are.

- The type of personal information to use - we chose Home/Family. The selected personal information can be edited by pressing the **Update** button.

Pressing the **Finish** button on the last dialogue box, causes the Wizard to display the screen shown below which has two panels, with the graphic on the right, and a menu of choices on the left.

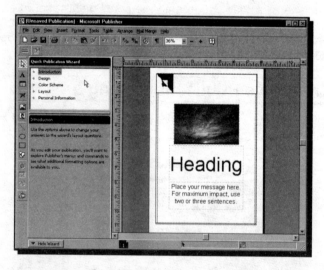

As you can see from the menu of available choices, it is possible to edit everything you have done so far, including the selection of an alternative page design. You can even change the graphic by double-clicking it, which displays the Insert Clip Art dialogue box with a selection of similar type of graphics to the one you are using.

Finally, note the different menus and Toolbars that appear on your screen as you select different parts of your work. For example, selecting a Picture Frame, displays a different Formatting Bar from the one displayed when a Text Frame is selected, as shown below.

The Formatting Bar

As we have seen previously, the buttons on the Formatting Bar change depending on which object you have selected. When a Picture Frame is selected, the buttons on the Formatting Bar have the following functions as described below.

Crop Picture

Wrap Text to Frame

Wrap Text to Picture

Fill Colour

Line Colour

Line/Border Style

Picture Frame Properties

Rotate Left

Rotate Right

Flip Horizontal

Flip Vertical

Crop Picture   Click the picture to select it, then click the **Crop Picture** button. Position the mouse pointer over one of the frame handles until the mouse pointer changes to Crop Picture shape, then drag the handle to trim the picture. Click the **Crop Picture** button once more to turn the feature off.

Wrap Text to Frame	Click the frame or shape to select it, then click the **Wrap Text to Frame** button.
Wrap Text to Picture	Click the picture to select it, then click the **Wrap Text to Picture** button.
Fill Colour	Click the object to select it, then click the **Fill Color** button. Click **Fill Effects** for more options.
Line Colour	Click the line to select it, then click the **Line Color** button. Click **More Color Schemes** for more options.
Line/Border Style	Click the line or border to select it, then click the **Line/Border Style** button. Click **More Styles** for more options.
Picture Frame Properties	Click a picture to select it, then click the **Picture Frame Properties** button. On the displayed dialogue box you can select text wrapping options and margins.
Rotate/Flip	The two rotate and two flip buttons rotate/flip a selected Picture frame in the direction indicated by the respective buttons.

Finally, when a Text Frame is selected, the buttons on the Formatting Bar have functions associated with text formatting. For that reason, they are similar to the ones displayed when working with a Microsoft Word document. For details of their function see Chapter 6.

The Objects Tools

When a Picture Frame is selected, the Objects Tools buttons display to the left of your screen. These buttons have the following functions:

Pointer Tools

Text Frame Tool

Table Frame Tool

WordArt Frame Tool

Picture Frame Tool

Clip Gallery Tool

Line Tool

Oval Tool

Rectangle Tool

Custom Shapes

Hot Spot Tool

Form Control

HTML Code Fragment

Design Gallery Object

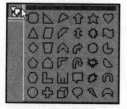

The function of most of the Objects Tools are self-evident. They allow you to create various frames and different shapes, including Custom Shapes, as shown here, and a selection of Design Objects. Finally, you can use the Web tools to create a hot spot, form control, or HTML code fragments. For these and other design tools, look up the **Publisher Tutorial**, to be found under the **Help** menu option.

Saving your Work

If you use Publisher for more than half an hour, the following
warning box will appear on your screen, asking you to save
your work.

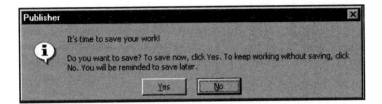

Clicking the **Yes** button, or if you are quicker off the mark and
used the **File, Save** command, the following dialogue box is
displayed.

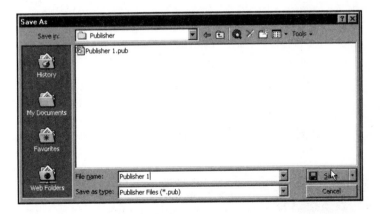

As usual, we have created a folder within **My Documents**
folder to hold our Publisher work. Save your design under the
filename **Publisher 1**. The extension **.pub** is automatically
added by the program so that Publisher can distinguish this
file as its own.

Opening an Existing File

To Open an already saved file when first starting Publisher,

click the **Existing Files** button at the bottom of the Publisher Catalog screen, the left pane of which is shown here. If on the other hand you are already working with Publisher and want to open a different file, then click the Open button, shown here, on the Standard Toolbar.

Whichever method you use, Publisher displays its Open dialogue box, as shown below.

To open a saved file, navigate to the folder in which you saved your work (ours is the Publisher folder created within the My Documents folder), and either highlight the required file and click the **Open** button, or simply double-click it.

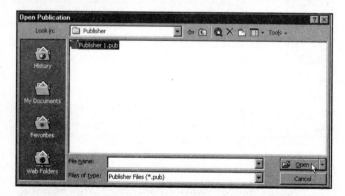

We suggest you open the file **Publisher 1**, which we saved earlier, and practice moving its frames, re-sizing them, adding your own text. Publisher guides you throughout - it couldn't be simpler. Try it.

Creating a Blank Publication

You create a blank publication if you want Publisher to set the dimensions of the publication, but you want to specify your own text and design. To do this, restart Publisher, so you can get to the Catalog screen, then click the Blank Publication tab, as shown below.

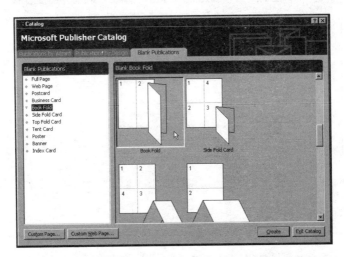

As you can see, there are several page set-ups to choose from, including some that require folding. These type of publications print pages on one sheet of paper that can be folded into a booklet.

To illustrate the process, select the Book Fold publication and click the **Create** button. Publisher displays the following dialogue box, informs you how many pages are available in the built-in design and asks you whether you would like to add more.

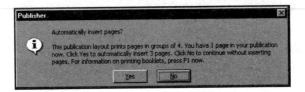

In the same warning box, it is also suggested that you press the **F1** function key for help with printing folded booklets. Doing so, displays the following help screen, which we suggest you look at closely if you intend to create and print such publications.

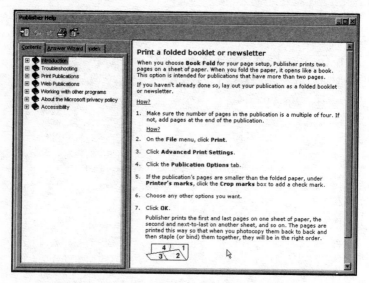

When you finish creating a blank publication, the Quick Publications Wizard allows you to change its design, colour scheme, and layout, in the same way as when you created a publication using a standard design Wizard.

Multiple Page Publication

If you have more than one page in your publication, Publisher

displays page icons at the bottom of the screen. You can use these icons to navigate through your publication.

If you need to add more pages to a publication, use the **Insert, Page** command. Pages can be added before or after the current page using the dialogue box.

Printing your Work

There are three ways to print and reproduce a publication using Publisher. These printing methods depend on the type of reproduction and quality you require.

- Use a desktop printer for a limited number of copies provided the quality of your printer meets your needs.

- Use a copy shop for a large quantity of copies at an economic cost. The quality will be better than most desktop printers.

- Use a commercial printing service when you want the highest quality printing. For large runs, commercial printing costs can be competitive with copy shops. Using a commercial printing service requires you to take your files with you.

Before you print your work on your desktop printer, make sure that you have an adequate supply of the type and size of paper your publication requires. Then use the **File, Page Setup** command to display the dialogue box shown below.

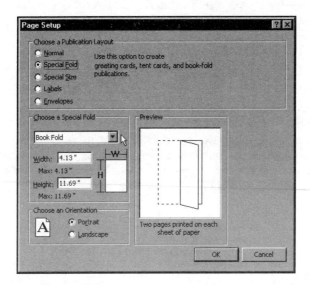

As you can see, depending on the design of your publication, the Page Setup dialogue box reflects the appropriate printing requirements. Make your specific selection and press **OK**, then use the **File, Print** command (or press the **Print** button on the Standard Toolbar), to begin printing. However, before printing your work, don't forget to spell check it, then preview it. It might save a few trees!

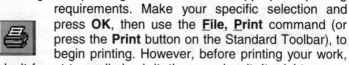

If you intend to have your publication printed at a copy shop or at a commercial printing service, find out their requirements before you start your design. Apart from the available paper size, you need to know the preferred method of delivering your work; take files on disc, send files via the Internet, or deliver a master copy. If you are required to take your files on disc, then Publisher can help with the **File, Pack and Go** command, which starts a Wizard to help you with your task.

Finally, you could use Publisher to design your very own Web site. Have a look at the Web Sites Wizard which helps you put together your requirements. Alternatively, you could design your own publication, then use the **File, Create Web Site from Current Publication** command. We leave this to you to try by yourself, as this is beyond the scope of this book.

* * *

Publisher is obviously capable of a lot more than we have introduced here, but you should now be in a position to explore more of the package's facilities by yourself. Try it and have fun!

* * *

16

Glossary of Terms

Address	A unique number or name that identifies a specific computer or user on a network.
Browse	A button in some dialogue boxes that lets you view a list of files and folders before you make a selection.
Browser	A program, like the Internet Explorer, that lets you graphically view Web pages.
Byte	A grouping of binary digits (0 or 1) which represent information.
Clipboard	A temporary storage area of memory, where text and graphics are stored with the cut and copy actions.
Command	An instruction given to a computer to carry out a particular action.
Configuration	A term referring to the way you have your computer set up.
Dial-up connection	A popular form of Internet connection for the home user, over standard telephone lines.
Default	The command, device or option automatically chosen by the system.
Disc file	A collection of program code, or data, that is stored on disc under a given name.
Document	A file produced by an application program.

Domain	A group of devices, servers and computers on a network.
Download	To transfer to your computer a file, or data, from another computer.
Drag	To press and hold down the left mouse button while moving the mouse, to move an object on the screen.
Drive name	The letter (followed by a colon) which identifies a floppy disc drive, a hard disc drive, or a CD-ROM drive.
File	The name given to an area on disc containing a program or data.
File extension	The optional, usually three-letter suffix following the period in a filename.
FTP	File Transfer Protocol. The procedure for connecting to a remote computer and transferring files.
Function	A built-in formula which performs specific calculations in a spreadsheet or database cell.
Function key	One of the series of 10 or 12 keys on the keyboard, marked with the letter F and a numeral.
Graphic	A picture or illustration, also called an image. Formats include GIF, JPEG, BMP, PCX, and TIFF.
Hardware	The equipment that makes up a computer system, excluding the programs or software.
Host	A computer acting as an information or communications server.

HTML	HyperText Markup Language; the format used in most documents on the Web.
Hyperlink	A segment of text, or an online image, that refers to another document on the Web.
Hypermedia	Hypertext extended to include linked multimedia.
Hypertext	A system that allows documents to be cross-linked so that the reader can explore related links, or documents, by clicking on a highlighted word or symbol.
Internet	The global system of computer networks.
Intranet	A private network inside an organisation.
IP	Internet Protocol - The rules that provide basic Internet functions.
ISP	Internet Service Provider - A company that offers access to the Internet.
Kilobyte	(KB); 1024 bytes of information or storage space.
LAN	Local Area Network; PCs, workstations, or minis, sharing files and peripherals within the same site.
Linked object	A place holder for an object inserted into a destination document.
Links	The hypertext connections between Web pages or documents.
Location	An Internet address.
Megabyte	(MB); 1024 kilobytes of information or storage space.

Megahertz	(MHz); Speed of processor in millions of cycles per second.
MIDI	Musical Instrument Digital Interface - enables devices to transmit and receive sound and music messages.
Multimedia	The use of photographs, music, sound, and movie images in a presentation.
Network	Two or more computers connected together to share resources.
Pixel	A picture element on screen; the smallest element that can be independently assigned colour and intensity.
POP	Post Office Protocol - a method of storing and returning e-mail.
Post	To send a message to a mailing list or newsgroups.
Processor	The electronic device which performs calculations.
Protocol	A set of rules or standards that define how computers communicate with each other.
Text file	An unformatted file of text characters.
Toggle	To turn an action on and off with the same switch.
TrueType fonts	Fonts that can be scaled to any size and print as they show on the screen.
Web Page	An HTML document that is accessible on the Web.
Zoom	Enlarged view focusing on a portion of a page so that you can see the fine details of your page layout.

Index

Companion Discs

COMPANION DISCS are available for most computer books written by the same author(s) and published by BERNARD BABANI (publishing) LTD, as listed at the front of this book (except for those marked with an asterisk). These books contain many pages of file/program listings. There is no reason why you should spend hours typing them into your computer, unless you wish to do so, or need the practice.

ORDERING INSTRUCTIONS

To obtain companion discs, fill in the order form below, or a copy of it, enclose a cheque (payable to **P.R.M. Oliver**) or a postal order, and send it to the address given below. **Make sure you fill in your name and address** and specify the book number and title in your order.

	Name	Price	Price
BP		£3.50	
BP		£3.50	
Book No.		£3.50	
Name		Sub-total	£..........
Address		P & P (@ 45p/disc)	£..........
....			
....			
		Total Due	£..........
Send to: P.R.M. Oliver, CSM, Pool, Redruth, Cornwall, TR15 3SE			

PLEASE NOTE

The author(s) are fully responsible for providing this Companion Disc service. The publishers of this book accept no responsibility for the supply, quality, or magnetic contents of the disc, or in respect of any damage, or injury that might be suffered or caused by its use.